OSPREY COMBAT AIRCRAFT · 78

F4U CORSAIR UNITS OF THE KOREAN WAR

SERIES EDITOR: TONY HOLMES

OSPREY COMBAT AIRCRAFT • 78

F4U CORSAIR UNITS OF THE KOREAN WAR

WARREN THOMPSON

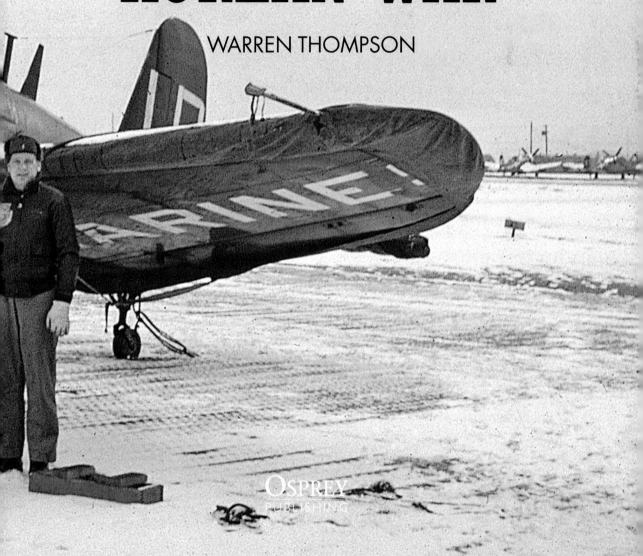

OSPREY
PUBLISHING

Front cover
Amongst the F4U pilots to see action during the early, critical, phase of the Korean War was 1Lt Vance 'Bud' Yount of VMF-323, embarked in USS *Badoeng Strait* (CVE-116) and then USS *Sicily* (CVE-118). He flew many missions against enemy troop concentrations in 1950-51. From the time the 'Death Rattlers' entered combat, its pilots were pushed to the limit due to the sheer number of targets in-theatre. They included the retreating remnants of the NKPA, as well as fresh Chinese troops pouring in during the winter of 1950-51. Yount remembered one mission in particular in the spring of 1951;

'We were told to attack a group of soldiers holding ground up around the village of Uijongbu, in South Korea. We carried a maximum load of bombs, rockets and 20 mm ammo. Our division pressed home the attack and scored excellent hits all over the area where the troops were clustered. Starting my final bomb run, I made a stupid statement that I thought I'd seen something on the next ridge, and was going to stay low after releasing my ordnance. This would give me a chance to check it out. Unfortunately for me, there was one very lucky rifleman who got a critical hit on my F4U. And it was in a vital place – my oil line!

'I felt the thud from the round as it hit. Suddenly, there was a puff of smoke in the cockpit, and I watched my oil pressure drop to 15 psi – normal was 80 psi. I yelled out that I'd been hit, and was turning to head south. One of the pilots in my division pulled up alongside me and said that he was going to stay with me, and that I should try and fly the aircraft back to the ship.

'I dropped a few degrees of flap as he flew under my tail searching for the oil leak. Naturally, with the sharp drop in pressure, I was sure that my oil cooler had been hit – it was located in a vulnerable spot. All the other gauges were normal, and the "big fan" out in front was still going around. If the engine quit, I had two choices – bale out or belly in. Baling out of an F4U was "iffy" at best, and many pilots had been hurt doing it, so I figured my best option was to set down in a flat place.'

In a situation like this, the pilot had to ensure that all his ordnance and external tanks had been jettisoned so as to reduce the risk of the aircraft flipping over or veering sharply in an undesirable direction on contact with the ground. In North Korea, suitable areas for emergency landings were few and far between, and narrow at best. Yount did exactly the right thing;

'My external tank went flipping through the air behind me, and I chuckled when my wingman got on the radio to see if that was me baling out. Everything seemed to be going according to plan as I flew closer and closer to friendly territory. As my good luck would have it, I was able to nurse it back to Suwon AB and land safely.

'Once the damage had been assessed, we found that a lucky shot had hit my oil pressure gauge, causing it to give me a false low reading. Fortunately, both my F4U and I were back in the war immediately, but it could have been a different story if I'd gone ahead and baled out before reaching a friendly base' (*Cover artwork by Gareth Hector*)

First published in Great Britain in 2009 by Osprey Publishing
Midland House, West Way, Botley, Oxford, OX2 0PH
443 Park Avenue South, New York, NY, 10016, USA
E-mail: info@ospreypublishing.com

Print ISBN 978 1 84603 411 4
PDF e-book ISBN 978 1 84603 871 6

Edited by Bruce Hales-Dutton and Tony Holmes
Page design by Tony Truscott
Cover Artwork by Gareth Hector using a model by Kevin Jongen
Aircraft Profiles by Mark Styling and profile commentaries by Tom Chee
Index by Alan Thatcher
Origination by PDQ Digital Media Solutions, Suffolk, UK
Printed and bound in China through Bookbuilders

09 10 11 12 13   10 9 8 7 6 5 4 3 2 1

For a catalogue of all books published by Osprey please contact:
NORTH AMERICA
Osprey Direct, C/o Random House Distribution Center, 400 Hahn Road, Westminster, MD 21157
E-mail: uscustomerservice@ospreypublishing.com

ALL OTHER REGIONS
Osprey Direct, The Book Service Ltd, Distribution Centre, Colchester Road, Frating Green, Colchester, Essex, CO7 7DW, UK
E-mail: customerservice@ospreypublishing.com

www.ospreypublishing.com

CONTENTS

INTRODUCTION

The Vought F4U Corsair earned its place in aviation history in the Pacific Theatre during World War 2. The Japanese had named it 'Whistling Death', and its aerial combat record was outstanding. Immediately after the war ended on 2 September 1945, most production contracts for propeller-driven fighters were cancelled and the emphasis placed instead on developing jet-powered aircraft for naval use. But things were a little different at Vought, where production of the F4U-4 version of the Corsair remained in full swing until mid-1947, by which time it had been supplanted by the vastly improved 'Dash-5'. Yet it was the F4U-4, available in large numbers, which was the most widely used Corsair variant during the war in Korea, particularly by the US Navy.

Five models actually saw combat in the first real conflict of the Cold War, namely the F4U-4, F4U-4B, F4U-4P, F4U-5N and the AU-1. There were several dogfights recorded between Soviet-built Yak-9 fighters and Corsairs early in the war, and Capt Jesse G Folmar even claimed a MiG-15 destroyed on 10 September 1952 while flying with VMF-312 'Checkerboards'.

These aerial clashes were the exception for Corsair pilots in particular, and naval aviators in general, during the Korean War, as they were fighting a new type of war vastly removed from that successfully waged against the Japanese in the Pacific five years earlier. During the latter conflict, most missions flown from US Navy carriers saw large formations of aircraft flying over a vast expanse of water to reach their targets. In Korea, naval aviators would fly relatively short distances from their carriers sailing in the Yellow Sea or the Sea of Japan to targets in the mountainous areas of North Korea.

Many of the missions flown by carrier-based Corsair squadrons were known as 'armed reconnaissance' sorties – a term borrowed from the USAF. These would typically see F4Us hunting for targets of opportunity in two- or four-aeroplane sections. As a rule, each flight would cover up to 70 miles of supply lines, both rail and road, in an effort to stop the enemy moving equipment and ammunition to the front. As an example, on one of the combat cruises made by the USS *Valley Forge* (CV-45), its Carrier Air Group Five (CVG-5) launched 3444 missions, more than half of which were armed reconnaissance sorties. The results were 2000+ enemy vehicles destroyed, including no fewer than 161 locomotives.

The key to US Navy and Marine Corsair operations was the wide variety of ordnance the aircraft could carry, and also the F4U's proven ability to 'get down in the dirt'. This was also the primary cause of the heavy loss rate suffered by Corsair units in Korea. The US Navy and Marine Corps had 389 F4Us destroyed (both in combat and operationally) whilst flying from carriers and more than 180 from shore bases.

In return, however, they inflicted enormous damage to the North Korean and Chinese military with their general purpose bombs, five-inch high-velocity aerial rockets (HVARs) and 0.50-cal and 20 mm guns.

Inside the cockpit of a well-worn US Navy F4U-4 Corsair in early 1951. Little had changed here in almost a decade of frontline service. Indeed. a naval aviator from World War 2 would have felt right at home in a Korean War Corsair (*Newmark*)

The ammunition belts load in 20 mm cannon-armed F4U-4s featured a mix of High Explosive Incendiary rounds, Armour Piercing rounds and standard Incendiary rounds. On occasion, the Corsairs also carried the huge 11.75-in (29.85-cm) 'Tiny Tim' rockets.

There can be no more genuine a tribute to the effectiveness of the Corsair in the close air support (CAS) ground-attack role than the thousands of soldiers and Marines willing to testify that the direct intervention of an F4U saved their lives – and, some would add, more than once. Indeed, with 46 percent of all US Navy/Marine Corps sorties in Korea being CAS, naval aviators had plenty of opportunity to come to the aid of 'grunts on the ground'.

Although the war was considered to be a jet-dominated one, the US Navy managed to commit a total of 29 squadrons of Corsairs to combat in Korea – a total that included detachments of photo-reconnaissance and nightfighter variants, as well as Reserve-manned units. The Marine Corps deployed six Corsair squadrons, one of which was a specialised nightfighter unit. This compares with the US Navy's 23 squadrons of F9F Panthers (including photo-reconnaissance aircraft) and the two Marine Corps units equipped with the jet-powered fighter-bomber.

Without the services of the large fleet of Corsairs built post-World War 2, the Korean conflict would have almost certainly taken on a totally different character.

EARLY DAYS

Shortly before dawn on 25 June 1950, a political nightmare was unleashed on the United States and the fledgling United Nations (UN) when North Korea invaded South Korea. The number of American troops in the Far East was totally inadequate to cope with this new crisis, although that was understandable since it was a post-war period and military strength had been drastically reduced in the years immediately following the ending of World War 2. The only recognised 'hot spot' in the world at that time was in Western Europe, where the aftermath of the Soviet blockade of Berlin had resulted in a significant increase in US and British troop levels in the region.

The only saving grace for the Americans in the Far East was their strong network of fighter wings based in Japan, the Philippines and on the island of Okinawa. There was also the 3rd Bomb Wing, with its World War 2-vintage Douglas B-26 Invaders. Neither the US Navy or the Marine Corps had a force in the region large enough to form an effective deterrent at the time of the North Korean invasion of the South, however, although this was quickly remedied when the *Essex*-class carrier *Valley Forge* was ordered to steam at full speed for the Sea of Japan.

CV-45 had begun a Western Pacific cruise on 1 May from its homeport of San Diego, and when the call came the ship was anchored in Hong Kong harbour. Within 24 hours the vessel was heading for Subic Bay, in the Philippines, to be provisioned, fuelled and armed. By 3 July it was in position to begin air attacks on North Korean targets. Later that same day, the war's first carrier strikes were mounted against North Korean airfields in and around Pyongyang by *Valley Forge's* CVG-5, supported by aircraft from the Royal Navy carrier HMS *Triumph* (R16).

July proved to be a pivotal month for all UN air units in Korea because the interdiction phase of the war finally started with a huge operation to close all the major road and rail links from Pyongyang to the frontline. While USAF B-29s destroyed the bridges, carrier-based Corsair, Skyraider and Panther units swept across the high traffic areas just north of the 38th Parallel.

On 22 July, USS *Boxer* (CV-21) docked in Japan with a cargo of 145 F-51D Mustangs gathered from USAF Reserve and Air National Guard units in the US. The carrier made the crossing at full speed because the USAF needed these fighter-bombers to provide relief for the hard-pressed US Navy and Marine Corps Corsair units. Until then, the F4Us had been the only

Valley Forge was the first US Navy carrier to respond to the North Korean invasion of the south. Its embarked air group, CVG-5, included two squadrons (VF-53 and VF-54) of F4U-4B Corsairs within its ranks. These VF-53 Corsairs are seen crowded together on the carrier's flightdeck awaiting their next mission (*W L Burgess*)

propeller-driven ground support types available in large numbers in the Far East. *Boxer* would begin its first combat cruise on 6 August with four Corsair units assigned to CVG-2 embarked.

In the meantime, CV-45 had been the sole US carrier on-station off North Korea since 3 July. CVG-5's two F4U-4B units were VF-53 and VF-54, and they had seen plenty of action by the time *Boxer* joined Task Force 77 (which controlled all carrier assets in the Korean War).

VF-54 pilot Midshipman Gordon E Strickland Jr provided an insight into conditions during those early July days when the pressure was on;

'When I landed back on my carrier after my first combat mission on 22 July, the public information officer informed me that this had been the first instance of a US Navy midshipman serving in combat since the Spanish-American war! I'd been flying with VF-113 back in the 'States when I was moved over to VF-54 for a combat tour. I only had about 180 hours' solo time in the Corsair, and 295 hours of total flying time.

'As I understand it, when the war started, the commanding officers of understaffed squadrons already in the Pacific sent an urgent request to Stateside squadrons for experienced pilots to fill the vacancies. However, the commanders of west coast squadrons had a different perspective. They were struggling to bring their own squadrons up to maximum combat readiness in preparation for imminent war cruises, and were naturally inclined to transfer those of their pilots who were not "advantageous" to their efforts. As I mentioned, I'd been with VF-113 for less than two weeks and was therefore very much an unknown and inexperienced entity, so off I went to bolster the fight in Korea.

'When I joined VF-54, I was very fortunate because of the quality of my fellow pilots and of my squadron CO and Executive Officer. I can

Corsairs from VF-54 are pictured here on *Valley Forge*'s flightdeck warming up their engines before moving to the take-off position. The 'S' tail code was used by both of CVG-5's F4U-4B squadrons. Parked immediately behind the Corsairs are AD-4s of VA-55 and AD-3Ws of VC-11 Det. At the very stern of the ship are F9F-3s of VF-51 and VF-52 (*W L Burgess*)

remember instances where both leaders made special efforts to smooth my way when, of course, they had a lot on their minds already. With this support, I went on to make a total of 26 combat sorties as a midshipman, before receiving my commission. When I finished my second tour with VF-54 aboard USS *Essex* (CV-9) in 1952, I'd flown a total of 118 combat missions. I'd earned, or at any rate been awarded, two Distinguished Flying Crosses (DFCs) and six Air Medals.'

Strickland and his fellow naval aviators in CVG-5 inflicted considerable damage on targets in the area around the 38th Parallel, as well as further north, using most of its complement of F4U-4Bs, F9F-3s and AD-4s. The enemy had not been expecting UN forces to attack targets in this area so soon, as most USAF efforts up until then had been concentrated in and around Seoul in connection with the evacuation of civilians from the capital. Units had also tried to hinder the North Korean People's Army (NKPA) as it drove south beyond the 38th Parallel.

In the vanguard of CVG-5's operations to provide critically-needed air support to the beleaguered Republic of Korea and US troops between 3 July and 19 November 1950 were VF-53 and VF-54. During *Valley Forge's* initial combat cruise with TF 77, its aircraft flew 5000+ combat sorties and delivered well over 2000 tons of rockets and bombs. These figures included the ordnance expended by the air group's two F9F squadrons and single AD-4 unit.

Despite such outstanding efforts in the air, the momentum on the ground remained with the North Koreans as they steadily pushed the UN forces back to the extreme southern tip of the Korean peninsula. If American air power had not been able to respond quickly, the war would soon have been over, at least on Korean soil. And although the UN

VF-114 and sister-squadron VF-113 served with CVG-11 during two war cruises aboard *Philippine Sea*. All their Corsairs displayed the letter 'V' on their vertical stabilisers. Those of VF-114 were identified by the yellow trim on the tip of the tail, propeller hub and drop tank. This photograph was taken during the early stages of the 1950-51 deployment (*Tailhook Association*)

controlled the skies, its ground forces were proving no match for the Soviet-equipped NKPA. The US Navy therefore wasted little time in providing back-up for *Valley Forge*.

USS *Philippine Sea* (CV-47), USS *Boxer* (CV-21) and USS *Leyte* (CV-32) were all rushed in from August 1950. CV-21's deck was crowded with F4U-4/4Bs from CVG-2's VF-23, VF-24, VF-63 and VF-64. *Philippine Sea* embarked F4U-4B-equipped VF-113 and VF-114 within CVG-11, while *Leyte* deployed VF-32 and VF-33 with its F4U-4s as part of CVG-3. This would be CV-32's sole combat cruise of the war, although the other carriers would return six times between them.

Philippine Sea represented an interesting case, because it was a relatively new carrier that had only made its shakedown cruise in the autumn of 1946. Prior to reporting to the Pacific Fleet, and before seeing combat in Korea, the carrier had undertaken another shakedown cruise in the Caribbean. The vessel had embarked so many distinguished guests during this period that the crew began to call CV-47 the 'Showboat', and the name stuck. It left Norfolk, Virginia, in late May, passing through the Panama Canal on the 31st. On 5 August *Philippine Sea* was designated the flagship of fast carrier TF 77, and it went straight into action.

CV-47 would subsequently remain on station for nearly 11 months, setting many combat records in the process, before returning home with CVG-11 – it set a new transpacific speed record during the latter crossing. *Philippine Sea's* second combat cruise began on 31 December 1951.

Most of the carriers operating off the North Korean coast established outstanding records with their air groups, almost all of which boasted at least one F4U squadron within their make up. By war's end, CVG-2 would be the most combat-experienced group of them all, having completed an unrivalled five deployments aboard *Boxer* (twice), *Essex*, *Valley Forge* and *Philippine Sea*. Enlisted armourer William Crouse of VF-64 recalled some incidents from the air group's first cruise, aboard CV-21;

'We departed San Diego on 22 August 1950. I was assigned to belt 0.50-cal ammunition. As we crossed the Pacific Ocean, our goal was to belt a million rounds, and this was to be done by the time we joined up with TF 77 in the Yellow Sea. We worked 12 hours on and 12 hours off, and stopped in Hawaii and at Sasebo, Japan, for personnel changes.

'The belting of a million rounds was achieved, only for it all to be shot off in the first week of air strikes! We were told that in three months of operations here we exceeded the total armament loads dropped by any US carrier in World War 2. Every third day we had to be re-armed at sea by supply ships – this took the better part of a day – as our ammo supplies were exhausted after just two days of flying.

'On the morning of 15 September I saw more ships joining our task force. These ranged from small vessels all the way up to battleships – it was the start of the Inchon landings. As our first air strikes were taking off, we were ordered to pull the 0.50-cal boxes out from the 02 deck to the catwalk to make it easier to arm the aircraft for the second strike.'

As the crews toiled, the aircraft involved in the first air strike were taking off from *Boxer's* flightdeck. Minutes into the launch, there was an explosion on the ship's bow. An F4U-4 (BuNo 96968) flown by Ens Jim Brogan of VF-23 had crashed off the port side and its fuel tank had blown up, creating a huge fire. Crouse continued;

'As the carrier passed the burning crash site, I saw Brogan swimming on the outside of the fire. The pilot and the fire were directly under our catwalk. I ducked to the back of the walkway to avoid the heat and smoke. My immediate reaction was "What if our ammo has some loose powder fragments?" As we cowered near the 0.50-cal ammo, the heat and smoke passed beneath us and was soon gone. Brogan was rescued and returned aboard by helicopter. He suffered minor burns and was flying in a week.'

Brogan himself recalled;

'My F4U warmed up in the pre-flight without incident. When it came time to take off, I gave it full power and the engine spluttered. My first thought was to brake hard, but the danger of flipping over didn't make that a good decision. I decided to crash to the left side of the ship. I was underwater when I cleared the cockpit, and well below the flames from the burning oil on the surface. From my underwater vantage point, I could see the edge of the fire, and I swam to the surface outside the fiery circle. The ship's hull passed close by me. I was hauled up and returned safely to the deck. The cause of the engine failure was thought to be in the spark plugs. Most of our F4Us had a new type of plug installed, but mine had the old ones.'

NKPAF

Intelligence reports, although skimpy at best, put the inventory of the North Korean People's Air Force (NKPAF) at 62 Il-10s, 70 Yak-series fighters, 22 Yak-18 transports and a small number of Po-2 biplane trainers. Most were based at two airfields near the capital Pyongyang and at Yonpo, on the east coast south of Hungnam. All these World War 2-era propeller-driven types had been donated by the USSR in the late 1940s, and only a few survived the first few weeks of the war. Those that remained serviceable duly fled to the safety of Manchuria.

At least 30 NKPAF aircraft were shot down by USAF F-82 Twin Mustangs and F-80 Shooting Stars in the first five months of the war, whilst US Navy Corsairs destroyed a large number of them on the ground in their revetments during the 3 July 1950 strike. The latter mission represented the first time since the end of World War 2 that carrier aircraft had destroyed enemy aircraft both on the ground and in the air – two Yak-9s fell to F9F-3s from CVG-5's VF-51. The latter unit and sister-squadron VF-53 were making history on this date, for their Panthers were the first jet-powered naval aircraft to participate in combat operations.

It is not clear to what extent the North Koreans were planning to transport equipment and troops along the coast by barge or boat, but a blockade by US Navy ships and carrier aircraft prevented any such movement taking place. Indeed, communist forces received no support from the sea at all due the non-existence of the North Korean Navy, so the carrier units were able to concentrate on attacking key targets both along the coast and further inland. Corsairs took a heavy toll of the enemy's efforts to move supplies by day, but the initial momentum was always with the invaders, and UN forces would be fighting a defensive battle until mid-September.

MARINE CORPS F4Us

There was no sizable force of Marines in the Far East in late June 1950, with most of the Corps' aircraft being stateside. However the reaction time of these units was extremely fast, for Marine Air Group (MAG) 33 was ordered to embark in USS *Badoeng Strait* (CVE-116), which was heading for Kobe, in Japan, in early July. Its three F4U Corsair squadrons were ready to fly their first combat missions by 3 August.

All three squadrons within the group were steeped in tradition following their outstanding contributions to victory in World War 2. The most famous were the 'Black Sheep' of VMF-214, followed by the 'Death Rattlers' of VMF-323 and VMF(N)-513's 'Flying Nightmares'. The latter unit provided MAG-33 with a nightfighter capability thanks to its radar-equipped F4U-5Ns – a type that had seen limited action in the latter stages of World War 2.

By mid-August, planning for a UN breakout from the Pusan perimeter was in its final stages. The plans would call for a maximum effort from Marine Corps ground forces as part of an amphibious landing at Inchon. The following month MAG-12 also arrived in-theatre with two squadrons of day fighter Corsairs, namely VMF-212 'Devilcats' and VMF-312 'Checkerboards'. With five Marine F4U units now primed for action, the combined strength of the two MAGs represented the Corps' biggest deployment since World War 2.

Operations were initially hindered by something as simple as a lack of accurate maps, however. Two years earlier, the USAF's 8th Photographic Reconnaissance Squadron had conducted extensive mapping of South Korea and some Pacific islands using the Northrop F-15A Reporter – a postwar development of the P-61 Black Widow nightfighter. Maps of North Korea were practically non-existent, however.

Fortunately, the Marine Corps had its own photo-reconnaissance units, although these were only in flight strength as the photo squadrons of the 1st and 2nd Marine Air Wings (MAWs) had been decommissioned in 1949 due to funding cut-backs. To maintain a photo-reconnaissance capability, each decommissioned squadron was divided into three separate units and these were individually assigned to each MAW. Flying the F4U-5P, one unit would be deployed with each MAG, and another assigned to the Headquarters Squadron of the 1st MAW.

MAG-33's photo detachment within the group was comprised of just two F4U-5P Corsairs, approximately 20 maintenance personnel and four pilots – Maj Don Bush, Capt Ed Ganschow, Capt Kenny Dykes and TSgt George Glauser. Both aircraft were quickly flown to Itami Air Base following the carrier's arrival in Kobe. MAG-33's attack Corsairs remained aboard the carrier, which then headed north for the Pusan perimeter to provide much needed support for a Marine Corps brigade that had been sent in to assist beleaguered UN troops surrounded by the NKPA.

As one of only four Corsair photo-reconnaissance pilots in-theatre at the time, TSgt George Glauser soon found himself in the thick of the action, as he recalls;

'Our immediate mission was to provide photo coverage of the North Korean movement toward the harbour city of Pusan. Every one of our sorties was directed by the USAF, and we provided photo intelligence of the enemy's movements along Pusan's 40-mile perimeter. These photos were sent daily to the Tokyo HQ of Supreme UN Commander, Gen Douglas MacArthur.

'All our initial air support missions were flown out of Itazuke AB, in Japan, and my first sortie took place on 10 August over the Pusan perimeter. These missions began before sunrise, and usually didn't end until after sunset. It was common to fly for up to eight hours during these sorties. I would depart Itami AB and land at Itazuke to receive briefings from the USAF. I then flew over the Sea of Japan to the Pusan area, where I would expose my film magazine, before flying back to Itazuke, debriefing and finally heading home to Itami. It was always a long day.'

TSgt George Glauser is helped with his straps as he settles into the cockpit of his F4U-5P prior to commencing yet another photo mission over Inchon harbour prior to the Marine Corps' daring amphibious assault on 15 September 1950. Glauser was assigned to MAG-33's photo detachment at Itami AB, Japan (*George Glauser*)

'The Corsair had a viewfinder in the floor, aft of the control column, which the pilot was supposed to use to help him align his aircraft with the target for the vertical aerial shots. I never used the window, however, because the Corsair's radial engine had a propensity for leaking oil, which would liberally coat the underside of the aircraft and totally obscure the viewfinder. I used the nose of the aircraft instead as my main alignment aid for each photo run.'

These photo-reconnaissance sorties lasted for just two weeks, at which point the advancing North Koreans were stopped at the Pusan perimeter by a blocking force of US Army, RoK and Marine Corps troops. Having finally stopped the NKPA in its tracks, Gen MacArthur and his staff devised an amphibious assault behind enemy lines that would trigger a UN offensive known as Operation *Chromite*. The strategic port at Inchon was selected as the target for the assault.

On 26 August MAG-33's small detachment of two F4U-5Ps received orders to begin flying missions from Itazuke to the Inchon area. Capt Dykes and TSgt Glauser were assigned this duty. The key to the success of the invasion was for UN planners to have sound information on the

VMF(N)-513 was one of the first three Marine Corsair squadrons to arrive in the Far East to participate in the war with MAG-33. This photograph was taken at Itazuke AB, Japan, just days after the unit had arrived in-theatre (*Roy Oliver*)

32-ft tides in the harbour. They desperately needed detailed photographs taken at various times of high, low and ebb tides of the entire harbour area, surrounding shoreline and the city of Inchon itself. To accomplish this, both pilots were tasked with flying eight missions over a period of four days. Glauser continues his story;

'Between 27-30 August I flew four solo missions out of Itazuke. After complete flight planning and coordinating with my USAF escorts, I proceeded by dead reckoning to fly out over the Sea of Japan, up the west coast of Korea and on to the port of Inchon. My time-on-target was only 20 minutes, which was more than enough for exposing an entire magazine of film on oblique shots, before returning to base.

Both the US Navy and the Marine Corps operated small detachments of photo-reconnaissance F4U-4/5P Corsairs, and these saw considerable action during the early months of the war. Here, MAG-33's TSgt George Glauser poses for the camera with his photo-Corsair at Itami AB, Japan (*George Glauser*)

'Fuel was always critical, as adverse winds, weather or encounters with the enemy could quickly lengthen your flight time beyond the allocated 3.5-hour limit. Upon arrival back at Itazuke, I would debrief with USAF Intelligence. The exposed film magazine was immediately flown back to Itami by courier, processed overnight and sent directly to MacArthur's HQ in Tokyo.

'Photographing the harbour and its surrounding areas required precision flying and split-second timing. I flew a precise box-like pattern at 2500 ft on all cardinal compass headings. My first run was on a southerly heading over the water. Each of the next legs necessitated a hard 90-degree turn, followed by immediately rolling wings level before the short eight-second intervalometer green exposure light came on for the next photo. Each succeeding turn to the new cardinal heading had to be precisely executed in that eight-second timed sequence. I also had to accurately calculate the number of exposures I could take on each leg due to the limited amount of film in the magazine. Finally, I had to keep my airspeed down, as anything in excess of 120 knots would result in fuzzy and blurred photos.'

Flying over the harbour at such a slow speed made Glauser's Corsair a sitting duck. Fortunately for him, the surviving NKPAF aircraft had long since fled to Manchuria, and there was very little in the way of anti-aircraft artillery (AAA) in the area. Glauser said he felt like a civilian pilot towing an advertising banner over a crowded beach on a bright sunny day. Nevertheless, the clarity of the film he and Dykes shot was outstanding, and it helped in planning and executing a perfect assault by the Marines on Inchon on 15 September 1950.

Throughout these missions, Glauser was escorted at low level by two F-82 Twin Mustangs from the 68th Fighter (All Weather) Squadron, based at Itazuke. Top cover was provided by four F-80C jets from the 8th Fighter Bomber Group. Glauser was duly awarded the DFC for his four photo-reconnaissance missions.

'HAPPY VALLEY' HEADS HOME

Valley Forge's first combat cruise ended on 1 December, its air wing having provided critically-needed air support when other UN aircraft had been pushed off the Korean Peninsula by onrushing communist forces that overran a succession of airfields and forced all shore-based units to pull back to Japan. At this point in the war, USAF units could only provide limited support from Japanese bases. The only on-call, short notice CAS came from aircraft carriers, with *Valley Forge's* CVG-5 in the vanguard.

During the vessel's last week on-station, the carrier's air group had seriously hindered the enemy's efforts to re-supply the large number of Chinese troops that were now overwhelming UN ground forces following the latter country's surprise entry into the war on 26 November 1950.

The sheer number of Mustangs and Corsairs working the interdiction routes had forced the enemy to start moving everything at night. This meant that at first light, the communists had to find ingenious ways of camouflaging the trucks that had survived the night bombing missions by UN aircraft. To counter this, the piston-engined fighter-bombers had to fly even lower to spot the well-hidden vehicles and ammunition dumps.

Results were even more effective for the Corsair units when they worked with an airborne controller. On one early-morning mission in mid-November, four US Navy F4Us were guided to a camouflaged truck park, which their pilots would probably not have spotted on their own. After several rocket and firing passes, the entire area was spewing flames and secondary explosions. Next, they were told to fly a short distance away to a small village. After making a firing pass, the huts exploded in flames and thick black smoke, which indicated a cache of petroleum-related material. During the war, Corsair pilots achieved countless successes against camouflaged targets such as these.

Amongst the F4U pilots to see action during this critical early phase of the war was 1Lt Vance 'Bud' Yount of VMF-323, embarked in *Badoeng Strait*. He flew many missions against enemy troop concentrations with the unit, which saw its first action on 6 August 1950. From the time the 'Death Rattlers' entered combat, its pilots were pushed to the limit because of the overwhelming number of targets. They included retreating remnants of the NKPA, as well as fresh Chinese troops pouring in during the winter of 1950-51. Yount recalled one mission in particular;

'We were told to attack a group of soldiers holding ground up around the village of Uijongbu. We carried a maximum load of bombs, rockets and 20 mm ammo. Our division pressed home the attack and scored some excellent hits all over the area where the troops were clustered. Starting my final bomb run, I made a stupid statement that I thought I'd seen something on the next ridge, and was going to stay low after releasing my ordnance. This would give me a chance to check it out. Unfortunately for me, there was one very lucky rifleman who got a critical hit on my Corsair. And it was in one of the most vital places – my oil line!

'I felt the thud from the round as it hit. Suddenly, there was a puff of smoke in the cockpit, and I watched my oil pressure drop down to 15 psi – normal was approximately 80 psi. I yelled out that I'd been hit, and was turning to head south. One of the pilots in my division pulled up alongside me and said that he was going to stay with me, and that I should try and fly the aircraft back to the ship.

'I dropped a few degrees of flap as he flew under my tail searching for the oil leak. Naturally, with the sharp drop in pressure, I was sure my oil cooler had been hit – it was a very vulnerable spot. All the other gauges were normal, and the "big fan" out in front was still going around. If the engine quit, I had two choices – bale out or belly in. Baling out of an F4U was "iffy" at best, and many pilots had been hurt doing it, so I figured my best option was to set down in a flat place.'

In a situation like this, the pilot had to ensure that all his ordnance and external tanks had been jettisoned so as to reduce the risk of the aircraft flipping over or veering sharply in an undesirable direction on contact with the ground. In North Korea, suitable areas for emergency landings were few and far between, and narrow at best. Yount did exactly the right thing;

'My external tank went flipping through the air behind me, and I chuckled when my wingman got on the radio to see if that was me baling out. Everything seemed to be going according to plan as I flew closer and closer to friendly territory. As my good luck would have it, I was able to nurse my F4U back to Suwon AB and land safely. Once the damage had been assessed, we found that a lucky shot had hit my oil pressure gauge, causing it to give me a false low reading. Fortunately, both my Corsair and I were back in the war immediately, but it could have been a different story if I'd gone ahead and baled out before reaching a friendly base.'

CARRIER PHOTO-RECONNAISSANCE

For quite some time, the only available carrier-borne photo-reconnaissance aircraft in Korea were a handful of F4U-4Ps assigned to the various VC-3 and VC-61 detachments. They were eventually supplanted in November 1950 by the F2H-2P Banshee and F9F-2P Panther jets of VC-61, which provided the US Navy's photo-reconnaissance capability for the rest of the war. The F4U-4Ps were deployed in a similar manner to the F4U-5N nightfighters, with a small detachment operating from various carriers. Their work was critical to target selection, and also to the Inchon landings. Lt(jg) Ray Hosier was one of the VC-61 pilots who saw action in the very early stages of the war from the deck of *Philippine Sea*. He described the sequence of events leading up to his combat missions;

'We departed North Island, en route to Hawaii, on 5 July 1950. By the 10th of that month we were flying the F4U-4P on training missions over Kahoolawe Island. This must have been our Operational Readiness Inspection, because by 2 August we were making practice strikes on Okinawa, and three days after that we were flying photo missions over targets in Korea, including Inchon, Kunsan, Mok Po, East Seoul, Sinanju and Anju. This was during the bleak days of the Pusan perimeter.

'My logbook shows that on 6 August I flew into Taegu AB within the perimeter to pick up some evacuation information. I then delivered it to the flagship, *Valley Forge,* and flew back to "Phil Sea".

'Throughout my tour, our missions were mostly against assigned targets, where we would shoot verticals and obliques. The next day, the air group would strike them, and we would come in behind them to do the post-strike pictures and record the damage. We were also covering the

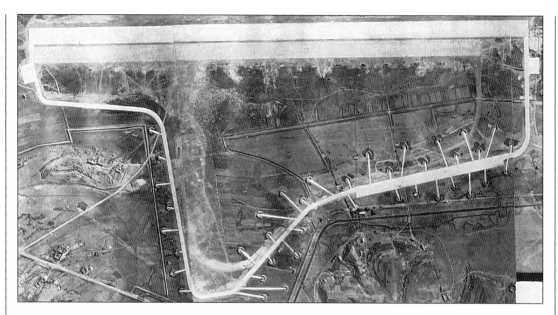

Lt(jg) Ray Hosier of VC-61 took this unauthorised photo of Antung air base from his F4U-4P during the autumn of 1950. He was jumped by a MiG-15 as he left the area, but was able to elude it at a very low altitude. This was before the MiGs started behaving aggressively, and also prior to the arrival of USAF F-86 Sabres in-theatre (*Ray Hosier*)

Inchon landings. Mine was the first aeroplane to land at Seoul's Kimpo AB on 18 September immediately after the Marines had captured it back from the North Koreans. There were bodies of enemy soldiers scattered all over the field. Less than two weeks after Inchon, I photographed a six-strip map of Pyongyang at 16,000 ft while drawing some AAA!'

On some of the photo missions the F4U-4P Corsairs were armed with 800 rounds of 20 mm ammunition for their four wing-mounted cannon. Usually, when they had completed their assigned photo runs, the pilots went after targets of opportunity. Locomotives were a favourite – a few were still running during the daytime in the early weeks of the war, but it was not long before all were operating after dark. Anything that moved north of the frontline was fair game for an F4U.

Hosier recalled a hazardous mission on 10 November 1950, when he had to get good photographs of Sinuiju, after which he decided to head north of the border to make unauthorised runs over the bridge at Antung, as well as its nearby MiG base;

'Anything in Manchuria was not on my assigned target list, but I did it anyway. I flew directly over the airfield at about 2500-3000 ft and got a perfect picture. At the time a lot of MiG-15s were based there, and one of them was up over the field at very high altitude when I made my photo pass. I kept one eye on him and the other on my altimeter as I ducked down low, heading south. The pilot was probably inexperienced because he made a firing pass on me, coming straight down. He missed me by quite a bit. Evidently his guns weren't bore-sighted for that range. He had to pull out way above me because I was down so low, and he probably had concerns about being able to recover if he continued the firing pass.

'One week after this mission, my squadron picked up two new F4U-5Ps from *Valley Forge*, which was returning home. This variant was 16 inches longer in the nose because of the supercharger, and it had cameras that rotated electrically – the ones we got were shy of the electronic gear that made the latter a possibility, however. Our F4U-4Ps were just about worn out by the time these aircraft arrived.'

PUSH TO THE YALU

PUSH TO THE YALU

The landing at Inchon on 15 September 1950 was undoubtedly the key move made by UN forces in the early stages of the Korean War. It resulted from a brilliant strategy engineered by Gen Douglas MacArthur and carried out by the Marine Corps, with air support from all three branches of the US military and other UN air assets. Once the enemy realised that the Marines were slicing across the peninsula east of Seoul, and that their main escape routes were going to be cut, pressure on the Pusan perimeter was relaxed and the NKPA began a mass retreat to the north. From then until the last week of October, UN ground forces advanced as far north as the Yalu River.

When the First Marine Division landed at Inchon, it was able to push rapidly inland. Fifth Air Force units were tasked to their limit attacking the retreating enemy forces just north of the Pusan perimeter and then working all the roads and railway lines south of the Yalu. On paper, this should have left 'First Marines' with less than ample air cover, but in reality coordination between US Navy carrier aircraft and Marine Corps Corsairs left no gaps in coverage. Indeed, the two were able to meet all the air support requirements of the division's CO, Maj Gen Oliver P Smith.

Enemy resistance crumbled in the face of this air power, especially when Kimpo AB was liberated. Once that was accomplished, the crossing of the Han River quickly followed. After that came close-in fighting to free the South Korean capital, Seoul. In a break from flying CAS missions, Corsair units also covered USAF and Marine Corps transports that alleviated an urgent shortage of aviation fuel and ammunition by flying in 1545 tons of vital supplies between 18 and 24 September.

By late October, UN ground troops had reached the Yalu, and the belief that they would be 'home by Christmas' was on most men's lips. For a while it looked like this rumour would indeed become reality, but the enemy still had a huge trump card to play. Pilots of USAF Mustangs and US Navy Corsairs that had been hitting targets in extreme northwest Korea were reporting numerous sightings of big troop movements south of the river. They did not appear to be North Korean forces. MacArthur placed no credibility in these reports, but they turned out to be correct.

During the last week of October, UN Intelligence reported that elements of at least 11 Chinese Army divisions were confirmed to be present in that area. They also made an educated guess that these forces were not volunteers, but regular troops. It was then that UN forces realised that the war was about to take a very different turn. On 26 November, following a series of isolated counter attacks by the Chinese People's Volunteer Army, a massive force attacked the forward positions of the Eighth Army along its entire front. From this point onward, F4U units would be heavily tasked with stemming the communist tide, as they could get in close to the action from their mobile aircraft carriers.

The second 'flattop' to arrive on-station off Korea was *Philippine Sea*, whose first of four cruises began on 5 July with CVG-11 embarked. The

latter included F4U-4B-equipped VF-113 and VF-114. VF-113 pilot Lt
Sam Wallace recalled what followed the Chinese entry into the conflict;

'On the day our Intel realised the war was going to be expanded by
North Korea's northern neighbour, I was flying in a division of four
Corsairs, and we were assigned to a forward air controller (FAC) up near
Anjou. At that time, I don't think any of us realised the Chinese were in
it. When we got there, we weren't able to contact him, and we didn't
know what the problem was. We had all of our ordnance, so we began
working our way south, flying low enough to seek out targets of opportunity. When we arrived just north of Pyongyang we contacted a FAC.

'Our load consisted of napalm, frag (fragmentation) bombs and plenty
of 20 mm ammo. We were directed to a suspected munitions dump near
a village crawling with enemy troops. They were very close to friendly
forces who were trying to make an orderly retreat against overwhelming
numbers of communist troops. After expending all of our bombs and
napalm on the village, we strafed the munitions dump until we were out
of 20 mm rounds. When we had done all we could, we headed back to our
carrier. There wasn't much resistance against us because the troops were
hiding as best they could. However, the story doesn't end there.'

The US Navy and Marine Corps F4U units and the USAF F-51
squadrons probably saved more lives among the ground troops than will
ever be known. It was only on rare occasions that the pilots had a chance
to come face-to-face with any of them. Two months after Wallace's
division worked over the village close to the frontlines, they were on
liberty at a hotel near Mount Fuji, in Japan.

One night, while at the bar, Wallace was approached by a US Army
lieutenant colonel who said that some US Navy Corsair pilots had saved
him at a particular location, and he described the action and gave a date.

F4U-4 Corsair pilots of VF-113 pose
on the flightdeck of *Philippine Sea*
during the carrier's marathon first
war cruise, which ran from 24 July
1950 through to 7 April 1951
(*Buzz Warfield*)

Wallace said his division had been there, and pointed out his skipper, who had been leading the mission. The officer went over and thanked him personally for what he had done. Of all the CAS missions flown by VF-113, this represented for Wallace and his fellow pilots 'the only time we ever had any after-action contact with the guys on the ground we helped'.

HUNG ORDNANCE

During the course of myriad ground attack missions flown by F4U units in Korea, most pilots got to experience the unpleasant, and often dangerous, scenario of 'hung' ordnance. Lt Sam Wallace remembered an incident when his Corsair was carrying what was to be regarded as one of the most effective weapons of the Korean War – napalm. Communist troops feared it more than any other weapon used by UN attack squadrons in the conflict;

'On a mission near Hamhung, I was in a group hitting the last targets of the day. When we had finished our strikes, I ended up with one of my napalm tanks hung. I made at least a dozen passes attempting to get it to release it, but to no avail. As we left the beach on the way back to the ship, I made one more run in an effort to get rid of it. Miraculously, it let go. This was to my good fortune, as what do you do with an aeroplane preparing to land on a carrier that still has napalm attached? There would be no way that I'd be allowed to land on the deck and turn it into a fiery inferno.

'This mission was being flown in November, and the weather in Korea had already turned very cold. I'd have had a choice of flying far to the south to a friendly airfield or baling out, at night, close to the carrier and taking my chances in that cold water. I was very fortunate that the bomb let go when it did, thus averting a possible tragedy.'

Having supported the push to the Yalu, CVG-11's units then assumed a heavy burden in protecting the Marines as they fought their way back south during the Chosin Reservoir campaign. However, not all the US Navy's on-station F4U units were required to support retreating UN forces. The second priority during late November was to put pressure on the Yalu bridges across which Chinese manpower and supplies were being funnelled to the south. VF-113 pilot Ens Robert Horton flew several missions over the Yalu after the Chinese had started their first push into North Korea, and prior to the large-scale invasion of 26 November;

'My air group was assigned a maximum effort mission on 21 November. We were to destroy a major bridge spanning the Yalu River, and also take out all the AAA positions near Sinuiju. It proved to be a bad day for me and, as a matter of fact, the entire month of November nearly turned out to be my "Waterloo". My F4U was armed with the usual load of 20 mm rounds, 5-in HVARs and one 500-lb VT-fused bomb. Mid-way through the bombing run, while encountering some ferocious AAA, I felt a bump and a "whoomph", and realised my Corsair had taken a direct hit in the starboard wing. Suddenly, I was experiencing inverted flight.

'My immediate reaction was to throw my liberty hat over the side and then go out after it. However, being a devout coward, I decided not to because I'd been told that shore liberty wasn't too good in that area at that particular time!

'As my airspeed was around 340 knots, it took both hands on the control column to return my wounded Corsair back to something like normal flight. Why that 500-lb bomb didn't detonate and permanently end my aspiring career remains a mystery to me. I had the throttle "two-blocked", and I was flying up the Yalu River all by myself with everyone on the ground throwing everything they could up at me. I was still busy trying to keep my aircraft right side up. Suddenly, I realised I still had the bomb on board, so I quickly dumped it, hoping it would hit a nice juicy target on the ground. Whether it did or not, I'll never know.'

Now Horton's big problem was the shape his F4U would be in when it came time to make his arrested landing back aboard the carrier. In an effort to gauge the aircraft's ability to withstand the jarring impact of a flightdeck recovery, Horton went through a simulated landing at 10,000 ft – everything seemed all right. He was being escorted by his CO, Cdr John T O'Neil. Horton continued;

'As I accelerated the aircraft tended to roll to the right above 170 knots, so I settled on 160 knots and it flew right on in to the deck and I caught the No 3 wire. As I taxied up the flightdeck, I folded the wings and waved to all the guys up on the "ghouler's" bridge through the bathtub-sized hole in my right wing. My Corsair was flying the next day with a new right wing – a real tribute to the squadron's maintenance folks.

'Little did I know that I would have a much more serious problem when I had to make an emergency landing on *Leyte* six days later.'

During the month of November 1950, the US Navy lost only two Corsairs. One of them went down on the 21st and the other was lost on the 28th. These represented the US Navy's 32nd and 33rd F4U losses of the war to date. The Marine Corps lost 11 Corsairs (the 30th to the 40th) during the same period. These losses were minor compared to what lay in store when the Chinese started moving large-calibre AAA batteries south in significant quantities in 1951-52.

On 27 November 1950 Ens Horton almost became a statistic himself during a reconnaissance mission with his division south of Sinuiju;

'During our search, I spotted three trucks and was told to lead the attack on them. Because of the bitter cold my 20 mm cannon wouldn't fire, so I chose to drop some bombs on them instead. The trucks were in a valley with steep hills on either side. After completing my run, I was hit in the upper left of my back near my shoulder blade by ground fire whilst pulling up. It felt as if someone had hit me with a baseball bat, and I was thrown violently forward against my shoulder straps. A few minutes later, my left arm started to grow numb.

'I immediately radioed that I'd been hit, but discovered I couldn't transmit, although I could receive. My division leader and squadron executive officer, Lt Cdr Leo McCuddin, suggested that I should return to the carrier with him flying wing escort. During this time my arm had grown so numb it was practically useless. My problems grew much worse when we discovered that *Philippine Sea* was in the middle of a very heavy snow storm.'

Indeed, the weather could hardly have been worse. By the time Horton was overhead the carrier group, he had to begin his descent on instruments, breaking through the cloud base less than 100 ft above the water. He made a turn to port of about 90 degrees, and stayed on that heading until he spotted a slick on the water. This indicated the recent presence of a large ship. He followed the slick, hoping to find a carrier –

he didn't care which one, because he knew he needed immediate medical attention as he was getting weaker by the minute. But Horton was in luck;

'All of a sudden, the fantail of *Leyte* came into view. I flew along the starboard side, looking up along the flightdeck. Lt Cdr McCuddin informed the carrier that he was escorting a wounded pilot who needed to come aboard. Permission was given as the flightdeck was clear. It was only later that I found out that it was *Leyte*.

'As I made my final approach, I realised I had to climb to land safely on the deck. As I entered the groove, I broke a vial of ammonia, which kept me alert during the critical phase of my approach and landing. I was lifted from the cockpit and taken to the sick-bay, where doctors attempted, unsuccessfully, to remove the bullet from my back. To this day it remains inside me, but the only time it bothers me is when there's a sudden change in temperature. After 51 days of medical recovery aboard ship, I was returned to flight status and continued to fly combat missions.'

The evacuation of UN troops from North Korea with most of their equipment was successful. The Marines fought their way through tens of thousands of Chinese troops around the Chosin Reservoir in bitterly cold conditions. From the beachhead at Hungnam, 105,000 troops, 98,000 civilians, 350,000 tons of cargo and more than 17,000 vehicles were safely evacuated. Both sea and air assets supported the evacuation, which took place 24 hours a day.

These statistics, from the Bureau of Naval Personnel, do not, however, reflect the critical coverage provided by US Navy, Marine Corps and USAF aircraft. They constantly pounded Chinese positions between 12 and 24 December, when US Navy and Marine Corps F4Us played a significant role by flying CAS missions at treetop height.

When the major Chinese offensive opened on 26 November, its sole intention was to push UN forces off the Korean peninsula. The manpower was certainly available to complete this task, but the Chinese had grossly misjudged the potential of American air power. TF 77 took a heavy toll of Chinese troops, and their equipment, during the first week of the communist offensive, the air groups from *Philippine Sea* and *Leyte* flying round-the-clock interdiction missions south of the Yalu River. VMF-323, embarked in the light carrier *Badoeng Strait*, also played its part. As the situation deteriorated, two more large carriers arrived, namely USS *Princeton* (CV-37) on 9 December and *Valley Forge*, which commenced its second war cruise in mid December. Including the Marine Corps unit, TF 77 force could field ten Corsair squadrons by Christmas 1950.

All of these units were urgently required to help stem a Chinese breach in the lines defended by RoK forces. The latter were in danger of being overwhelmed by vastly superior numbers, and the frontline started to sag. *Philippine Sea* and *Leyte* used everything they had to help stave off the gathering momentum of the enemy forces flooding in from Manchuria. Up until the Chinese invasion, most naval air strikes had concentrated on the Yalu bridges, and the area around them. Many photo-reconnaissance missions were also flown, and aircraft also had to be provided for combat air patrols over TF 77. However, with UN forces now in danger of being wiped out by Chinese troops, CAS missions in direct support of retreating UN forces became the order of the day.

Occasionally this meant hitting targets in Manchuria, which had previously been categorically out of bounds for UN pilots. VF-32 F4U-4 pilot Lt Frank Cronin, who was heavily involved in this critical phase of the war whilst flying from *Leyte* with CVG-3, recalled;

'Before the Chinese entry into the war, our cockpit maps of the area bordering Manchuria and the Soviet Union had 20 miles physically cut off them. This had been done just in case an aeroplane went down near the border. The pilot would then be able to show his Chinese captors that he was lost and hadn't meant to violate their border.'

Lt Frank Cronin poses in the cockpit of his VF-32 Corsair on board *Leyte*. He was one of the pilots who helped cover Marine Corps ground forces when they fought their way through the massed ranks of the Chinese army around the Chosin Reservoir on their way to a successful evacuation in December 1950 (*Frank Cronin*)

The Marine breakout and retreat from the Chosin Reservoir under great pressure from the enemy is one of the most publicised campaigns in the Corps' history. It was successfully achieved with a minimum of casualties during the sub-zero weather typical of North Korea at that time of year. All F4U pilots, whether US Navy or Marine Corps, were aware that CAS was critical to the troops as they fought their way to the coast. Getting their F4Us down as low as possible to increase accuracy was crucial to the effectiveness of these missions. There was, however, one exception. Napalm could not be delivered below treetop height if pilots wanted to get home safely.

Lt Cronin recalled a harrowing mission that he flew on the morning of 3 December in support of the Chosin Reservoir breakout;

'I was scheduled to lead a flight from *Leyte* that comprised four F4Us and four AD-3s from VA-35. We were to work an area in the far northeastern part of North Korea. At that time, TF 77 was operating about 50-75 miles off the east coast from the Wonsan and Hungnam areas. When we launched, the carrier was approximately 100 miles from our target, sailing in clear weather with excellent visibility. However, before we reached the coast we ran into increasing cloud cover that topped out at 9000+ ft, forcing us to climb to 10,000 ft. We hoped that

During the UN advance to the Yalu River in the late autumn of 1950, Corsairs and Mustangs briefly operated from captured North Korean airfields such as Yonpo (K-27), where this VMF-212 F4U-4 is seen being serviced between missions in early November (*Dick Penrose*)

the weather over the target would be better, allowing us to descend to a lower level, where we could view enemy positions and pick out targets. But this was not to be. It was solid cloud cover with not a break in sight.

'The mountains in that area of North Korea topped out at over 8300 ft, with one in Manchuria reaching beyond 9000 ft – since we couldn't see any peaks, the clouds had to be rather thick. Especially critical was the fact that since leaving *Leyte*, we hadn't had a single navigational fix! If we'd had clear weather going in, we'd have been able to note where and when we crossed the coastline. Furthermore, there were no navigational aids in North Korea. That left only the little plotting board on my right knee and the weather briefing on the carrier before take off to estimate where we were.'

Forecast winds for various altitudes and locations are not always accurate, even today. Cronin had no idea where he and his two divisions were. With little or no chance of descending through the solid cloud cover, he told the other pilots he intended to make every effort to reach the Chosin Reservoir and help the embattled Marines. The knowledge that the enemy was pressuring them unmercifully kept all pilots focused on the mission regardless of the weather. Cronin continued;

'The situation required a bit of navigating with my trusty plotting board while flying my Corsair at the same time. That wasn't always easy for such a big change of direction and area, so I told the formation to fly loose while we made a wide circle. I went into "the plotting office" to try and figure out a new course to the Chosin Reservoir. My estimate – or guesstimate – was that Chosin lay 175 miles away in a southwesterly direction. It would take us about 50-60 minutes to reach the target area.

'Having done as much as I could, I sat back, passed the lead to my "Guardian Angel" and followed her. As matter of fact, the title to this story should be "Angels over the Chosin".'

While making these corrections and changing headings, the Skyraider leader asked the F4U division to slow down because his aircraft were having difficulty holding formation due to the Corsair's higher cruising speed. For the rest of the flight to Chosin, the cloud remained solid, topping out at more than 8000 ft, with no breaks in sight. After a while, Cronin began to consider the possibility that the force might not be able to find its way through the overcast to aid the troops at Chosin. Returning to the carrier would be another concern. He continued with his story;

'Some time later, what seemed to be a dark spot on the white blanket turned out to be a very small hole in the cloud cover, so we circled to investigate. To me, it looked about the size of a quarter, and after a couple of circuits, I could see what looked like water – frozen or not – at the bottom of a long tube. I sent my wingman, Ens Marty Goode, to see if he could identify the place, and to find out about cloud conditions in the area. I questioned whether we would have sufficient visibility and cloud clearance around the mountain tops. After what seemed like a long time, Goode came back up okay and said it wasn't the Chosin Reservoir, but the Fusen Reservoir. Now, for the first time since we took off, I was certain where we were.

'Chosin was only about 20 miles away, but the big question was would there be another hole in the clouds so that we could get down to help the Marines. A few minutes later we got out answer. A much larger hole was open right over the reservoir, and it was just big enough for four Corsairs followed by four heavily-laden Skyraiders.'

At that point, Cronin contacted a controller on the ground to tell him what loads they were carrying, and to receive targeting instructions;

'The controller was surprised, and pleased, to hear that we'd braved the harsh weather conditions to help them out of a tight spot. To get down through that hole we had to fly in very tight formation, with the wingmen's wingtips overlapping and slightly below the two flight leaders'. "Tail-end Charlie" flew slightly below and behind the lead aircraft. What with the very tight formation and the whirling props too close for comfort, it wasn't difficult for the pilots to concentrate on what they were doing. We successfully carried out many missions just like this one under ground control, using up all of our ordnance. Thankfully, we suffered no casualties or any hits whilst doing so.'

Although Cronin's two divisions had completed their bombing and strafing runs, they now faced the difficult task of returning safely to the carrier. The hole in the overcast was no more, and this prevented the Corsairs from climbing above the cloud-covered mountains. Fortunately, they were able to stay low and weave their way out below the cloud cover, hugging the ground all the way. The formation skimmed over Hagaru-ri and Kotori to Hamhung, then on to Hungnam and finally back to *Leyte*. Total time from launch to recovery was 3.5 hours.

Cronin, who attributed their good fortune during this mission in finding openings in the clouds to a 'Guardian Angel', was glad to be able to help the Marines on their march to the evacuation port. He was typical of most Marine Corps and US Navy fighter-bomber pilots of this period, who were determined to reach the Chosin area whatever the weather.

While the pilots were feeling their way to their targets and back to the carrier, the maintenance personnel were also battling the elements to pre-pare F4Us for the next mission. The enlisted Marines servicing Corsairs on snow-covered bases ashore often worked with just a tarpaulin over them, or in makeshift sheds. SSgt Jim McWilliams of VMF-312 at Wonsan AB recalled the harsh Korean winter of 1950;

Corsair maintenance at South Korean bases was performed under some of the crudest conditions. This F4U-4 from VMA-312 is being serviced out in the open between missions at Wonsan AB (K-25). Note the mud and water below the pierced steel plating on which the fighter is parked (*Jim Bailey*)

'At times it was so cold that we couldn't work on an engine with bare hands as our skin would stick to the metal. Engine oil got so thick that we built heaters out of gas drums and copper tubing using aviation fuel on the flightline to heat the oil before we could pour it into the engines. If I remember rightly, the F4Us had 33-gallon oil tanks and used an average of five to seven gallons of oil every time they flew. At night time, we eventually resorted to running the engines for 30 minutes every two hours so as to keep the oil warm.'

CHOSIN VETERAN

When the Marine Corps lists the most memorable and the most crucial battles in its history, Chosin Reservoir is always mentioned. Those involved faced two enemies – the Chinese hordes, who greatly outnumbered them, and the weather, which was the bitterest they had ever faced in combat. On top of that, the enemy always occupied the high ground, and bad weather made CAS missions difficult. Those fighter-bomber pilots who persevered will always be remembered by those who were on the ground. Amongst the former was VF-114, embarked in *Philippine Sea* with CVG-11. Ens Bill Redmon was one of the unit's pilots.

He had entered the US Navy in 1943, and was commissioned in 1945. Checked out in the Corsair in time to deploy to the Far East on 4 July (just days after the North Koreans crossed the 38th Parallel), Redmon recalled;

'We were on-station off the coast when the Marines were trying to break out at Chosin. We made it through the bad weather and were able to strafe the ridges overlooking the Marine columns, even though we couldn't really pick out any specific targets. The Chinese were all wearing white clothing, which enabled them to blend in with the snow and rendered them invisible to us.

'There were controllers on the ground with the Marines who directed us, and also informed us just how close we were to friendly troops when we dropped our weapons. Our most effective piece of ordnance was napalm, and that did more damage to the enemy that anything else.

'On 3 December 1950, one of our pilots made the mistake of dropping a 500-lb fragmentation bomb instead of his napalm from an altitude of about 50 ft when attacking troops near Chosin. His aircraft (F4U-4B BuNo 63041) sustained a lot of damage, and he had to make a forced landing at a very small airstrip nearby. The aircraft ran off the end of the runway, and as soon as the Corsair came to a stop, the pilot jumped out the cockpit straight into an icy stream! He then started running back in the direction of the airstrip, only to be warned that he had entered a minefield – a Marine had to escort him out. He was evacuated with the Marines on the last C-47 out that day, and was back on *Philippine Sea* within 24 hours.

'As a result of the Chinese entering the war, we spent nine months on that cruise. I flew 96 combat missions, and came back for a second tour on USS *Kearsarge* (CVA-33) in 1953 after becoming qualified as a landing signal officer.'

The most memorable event involving a Corsair in the Korean War took place just 24 hours after Ens Bill Redmon's experiences over Chosin. Two divisions of F4U-4s from VF-32 had been ordered to head into the same general area in an effort to ease the pressure on the beleaguered

Marines. Again, the weather was bad and the ground blanketed in heavy snow. One VF-32 aircraft (BuNo 97231) was being flown by the US Navy's first black fighter pilot, Ens Jesse Brown.

Attacking Chinese troops at low altitude, the Corsairs encountered a hail of small arms fire as they strafed communist forces found out in the open. Brown radioed that his F4U had taken a hit and was losing oil pressure. He had no choice but to belly in with wheels up, landing on the side of a snow-covered slope behind enemy lines near Koto-ri. For a few fleeting seconds it seemed that Brown had not survived the crash because his canopy remained closed.

Minutes later, Lt(jg) Thomas Hudner (in BuNo 82050) circled the site and saw that the canopy had now been rolled back. However, Brown was making no effort to climb out of the cockpit. He was either too badly hurt or he was trapped. As the other Corsairs concentrated on keeping the enemy troops away from the downed aircraft, Hudner decided that he would not leave his wingman behind. He would belly-in as close to Brown's Corsair as he could and attempt to free him from the wreckage.

Hudner successfully force-landed and quickly ran over to Brown's Corsair. It quickly became evident to him that Brown was badly hurt, and trapped by the cockpit instrument panel that had been pushed back into the pilot's legs during the crash. Hudner could not free Brown, so he rushed back to his own aircraft and radioed his still circling squadron-mates to notify the rescue helicopter's crew to bring an axe and a fire extinguisher, as smoke was now pouring from Brown's engine cowling. His hands were frozen stiff, and the only thing Hudner could do was don the extra cap and woollen scarf he carried on cold weather missions.

When the rescue helicopter arrived, its crew was also unable to free Brown. As night was falling, they had to take off without him. By this time Brown was unconscious, and his situation was deteriorating rapidly. Hudner departed with the helicopter, deeply upset that he had been forced to abandon his fellow pilot. In an effort to prevent the enemy from having access to the two downed Corsairs, and to Ens Brown, a flight of aircraft was launched to destroy the wreckage with napalm. For his valiant efforts to rescue a fellow pilot, Lt(jg) Hudner received his nation's highest award for bravery in combat, the Medal of Honor. Records state that these two aircraft were the US Navy's 35th and 36th Corsair losses of the war. A further 11 US Navy and Marine Corps F4Us would be lost to all causes before the year was out.

The statistics compiled by all branches of the US military in Korea between 25 June and 31 December 1950 show the degree of effort involved in stopping the North Korean invasion, and in finally turning the tide against them at Pusan. The USAF flew 95,886 sorties during this period, with 27,857 of them being CAS missions. The US Navy logged 16,854 sorties, while the Marine Corps added 12,827. The figures also show that 90 per cent of the Corps' sorties were to provide CAS for ground units. The US Navy's activity breakdown is reliably estimated at 25 per cent of sorties flown in defence of the carriers, 25 per cent on CAS and 50 per cent on interdiction missions. It should also be mentioned that protection of the carriers during this period was very important, as the number of surviving NKPAF aircraft was still unknown and a surprise attack on the fleet remained a possibility, therefore.

NAVAL OPERATIONS

During the Korean War, US Navy Corsair squadrons operated from no fewer than 11 *Essex*-class aircraft carriers, with Marine Corps units flying from six vessels classified as light carriers. Such a large number of ships ensured that three or four air groups were on-station at any given time from late 1950 onwards.

The pace of combat operations in-theatre following the Chinese invasion weighed particularly heavily on ships and air groups in TF 77 during the critical winter of 1950-51. One vessel more than any other felt the effects of this – *Valley Forge*. The first US carrier to respond to the crisis, the ship had finally been pulled out of the frontline and sent home in November after four months of near constant action. Arriving in San Diego on 1 December after deploying on 1 May, it just had time to swap CVG-5 for CVG-2 before heading westbound again on 6 December!

And like CV-45, CVG-2 already had a war deployment under its belt by then too, for it had returned to California aboard *Boxer* less than a month earlier. The air group flew myriad missions between mid December 1950 and late March 1951, with its trio of F4U-4 units (VF-24, VF-63 and VF-64) providing CVG-2 with its cutting edge.

Upon the completion of its cruise, VF-63 released figures to *Naval Aviation News* that represented achievements typical of

Below
Having just landed, this F4U-4 from VF-24 taxies towards the bow of CV-45. Several more aircraft from ATG-2 are in the pattern awaiting their turn to land. The group had deployed with no fewer than four F4U-4 squadrons (*Tailhook Association*)

Bottom
This section of Corsairs from *Valley Forge* comprises aircraft from VF-63 (foreground) and VF-64 (background). They are both carrying 5-in HVARs (*Jack Bucknum*)

Valley Forge undertook its second war cruise between December 1950 and April 1951 with four Corsair squadrons aboard, plus a nightfighter detachment. This VF-64 F4U-4 was a real combat veteran judging by the number of mission symbols painted beneath its cockpit (*Ralph Tvede*)

CVG-102's Intelligence Officer (smoking a cigarette) briefs VF-783 Corsair pilots in their ready room on their mission assignments for the day. The squadron served aboard *Bon Homme Richard* during its 1951 cruise (*Pete Colapietro*)

many F4U units flying from carriers with TF 77 at this time. During 1055 sorties, the unit's pilots had been credited with inflicting 2500+ enemy troop casualties, knocking out 11 T-34s, 27 gun positions, 50 vehicles and 18 fuel or ammunition dumps. These figures do not include a long list of other targets that were destroyed. Pilots also patrolled close to the coast, searching for enemy ships, and this resulted in several junks being sunk.

By the time *Valley Forge* was relieved by USS *Bon Homme Richard* (CV-31) in May 1951, the war had developed into something of a stalemate. The communists had been stopped and then pushed back to approximately the same position as the original 38th Parallel – the pre-war border between North and South Korea. However, the war still had a further 27 months of fighting to run before it finally came to an end. From now on UN air power would be focused primarily on interdicting Chinese supply convoys that were assigned the job of moving men and equipment to the frontline. Communist logistics personnel were tasked with keeping troops in direct contact with UN forces supplied with sufficient materiel to wage war on a daily basis. They were also told to stockpile supplies in North Korea to sustain potential future offensives.

UN ground forces were ordered to hold what territory they had, and the air arm was assigned the job of stopping all communist convoys and trains attempting to come south. Without supplies, the Chinese could not gain any momentum on the ground.

CV-31 found itself in the forefront of this campaign upon its arrival in TF 77. Its air group, CVG-102, included F4U squadrons VF-783 and VF-874, both of which were Naval Air Reserve units that had been mobilised for active duty. Many F4U pilots that saw combat during the war were reservists from all parts of the United States. Most had served in World War 2, and they were now needed once again because of their expertise in flying older propeller-driven types.

Aviation Electronic Technician Second Class Jettie Hill remembered VF-874's preparations for combat readiness, and its transition to the 'new' Corsair;

'My squadron was home-based at NAS Oakland, in California. It was called into active service on 26 July 1950, along with many other Reserve units. We'd been flying F6F

A VF-783 Corsair goes 'feet dry' over the North Korean coast as it heads inland in search of targets of opportunity. Its primary weapon on this mission is the 5-in HVAR (*Pete Colapietro*)

Hellcats when word came down that our Reserve squadron would be getting the Corsair. The F4U-4s that we received had been taken out of storage, and we were not at all familiar with them. They had to be thoroughly overhauled, new electronics installed and each aircraft flight tested as quickly as possible so that the pilots could get on with their flight training and bombing practice. This was a lengthy process that took until the spring of 1951 to complete. We then took *Bon Homme Richard* out for a shakedown cruise, as it too had just been re-commissioned. The aeroplanes flew out from San Diego for carrier qualifications.

'It took some time to get all of our pilots ready for the cruise, especially with a fighter that was new to them. I remember one night when they were out practicing and, as they lined up for landing on the "BHR", one of the aeroplanes was waved off. As he came around again, he flared out to touch down, and at the last moment remembered that his undercarriage was still up. As the landing gear doors opened, he touched down. There was relatively little damage to the aircraft other than to the gear doors.

'A short time later we loaded up and headed for Korean waters. Once we were on-station, our Corsairs were putting in long days, and our VC-3 night detachment was working until about 2300 hrs. Thirty days later we cut back on operations due to a shortage of ammo.

'When we started combat flying, we were told that our air group had the largest number of aircraft in operation of any carrier. We were replenished with food and fuel every four days or so. We had problems with some of our ordnance, specifically the "proximity bombs", as some tended to explode while still on the Corsair and others immediately after they were dropped. We lost a few pilots and aeroplanes that way.'

Bon Homme Richard sails at full speed from Japan bound for its operating station off the North Korean coast in early June 1951. The vessel's deck is crowded with F4U-4s from VF-783 and VF-874, together with AD-3s from VA-923 and F9F-2Bs from VF-781 (*Pete Colapietro*)

Members of Naval Reserve squadron VF-791 line up for an informal group photograph on the flightdeck of *Boxer* during the ship's 1951 war cruise. The squadron was stationed at NAS Memphis prior to being called to active duty (*Henry Champion*)

Boxer was one of the most active carriers committed to the war, undertaking four cruises in the Far East between August 1950 and November 1953. The vessel's 1951 deployment (2 March to 24 October) saw CVG-101 embarked, the air group including no fewer than four Naval Air Reserve-manned units within its ranks. VF-884 and sister-squadron VF-791 from NAS Memphis, Tennessee, duly became the first Reserve F4U units to see combat in Korea. The latter squadron had received its mobilisation orders on 20 July 1950 (less than 30 days after the North Koreans had crossed the 38th Parallel), and it left for NAS North Island, San Diego, five days later to be checked out in the F4U.

After many months of work-ups, VF-791 flew its first combat missions on 26 March 1951, and from then on it compiled a remarkable record. During its sole combat cruise, the unit destroyed or damaged 175 bridges, 140 trucks, 125 rail cars and 500+ buildings. VF-791 had expended 750,000 lbs of bombs and rockets, and it also took part in Operation *Strangle*, which was aimed at halting enemy supply movements to the south. Thanks to their dedicated maintenance personnel, each pilot averaged 60 missions. The unit totalled 1250+ sorties and 3600+ flying hours.

Lt(jg) Norman Edge participated in this deployment with VF-791's sister-squadron VF-884, based at NAS Olathe in Kansas. He undertook numerous CAS and interdiction missions from CV-21 in the spring and summer of 1951, with most of these sorties being flown at dangerously low altitudes. On some missions the pilots were able to take out assigned targets with a minimum of ordnance, leaving them free to hunt for targets of opportunity. However, many sorties ended in frustration, as Edge recalled;

'We went after our briefed target, and when we had levelled it we still

Lt George Denby of VF-884 is pictured at North Island, San Diego, in February 1951 prior to the squadron's departure aboard *Boxer* on the first of the unit's two combat cruises the following month. The 'Bitter Birds' of VF-884 compiled an impressive record during the squadron's time in-theatre (*George Denby*)

had something left. In my case it was napalm. There were only two of us – my flight leader and I – and as we skimmed over the terrain we saw this undamaged building standing all alone. Next to it was a machine gun, which was shooting at us, so we figured that the building must house something important. I lined up first, made my run and got what I thought was a perfect hit but nothing happened, as was often the case.

'My flight leader had followed me down so that he could shoot tracer rounds into the napalm canisters to ignite them if necessary. He failed to spot the point of impact, however, and didn't fire. I went back and fired a burst at the point I thought it had hit. Sure enough, the target ignited. It was a perfect drop, which landed about 20-30 ft in front of the building, but the structure remained unaffected. The bomb had hit the base of a huge stump and the napalm had splashed out on both sides in a V-shape. In the centre of the V stood the building, totally unscathed! The machine gunner and I traded shots. I think I got him, but I do know that he hit the leading edge of my right wing and the round exited back in the fabric. It was a close call.'

It was common knowledge that the North Koreans and Chinese did not use tracer ammunition. As a result, many US Navy and Marine Corps Corsair fighter-bomber pilots often only realised that they were being fired at when their aircraft was hit. A significant number of F4Us were also lost when they struck power lines whilst trying to avoid AAA. One such individual was a squadronmate of Lt(jg) Edge;

'I was airborne in another area when Lt W C Thomas was killed in action. He was flying lead in a flight that was hitting some targets when he

A VF-791 Corsair prepares to launch from *Boxer* in 1951. The squadron was identified by the white trim on the vertical stabiliser and propeller hub of its aircraft, as well as by the tail code 'A' (*Tailhook Association*)

VF-791 pilots practice formation flying off the coast of San Diego prior to departing on their combat cruise. The unit would fly combat missions from *Boxer* with CVG-101 between March and October 1951. This would prove to be the squadron's only Korean War deployment (*John White*)

VF-874 pilot Lt Herbert L Newmark receives congratulations from his plane captain after a dangerous mission over North Korea. His Corsair was hit several times, and the damage being indicated almost brought him down before he could return to the *Bon Homme Richard* (*H L Newmark*)

A 'Bitter Birds' Corsair from VF-884 prepares to launch from *Boxer* on a mission armed with seemingly ubiquitous 5-in HVARs (*John White*)

flew through power lines alongside a road. They pulled the arming wires from his VT-fused 500-lb General Purpose bombs. After flying the required 2500 ft to arm the fuse, the bombs exploded while they were still hung on his racks, blowing him and his aircraft to bits. I heard his last radio transmission, which was an attempt to warn the rest of his flight – "Watch out for the power li . . .", and he was gone. His wingman's gun camera film caught the explosion, as he was trailing Lt Thomas.'

VF-884's records show that it lost six of its original pilots in combat, together with two replacements. This was a high price to pay, but in return the unit delivered 740,000 lbs of bombs, 65,000 gallons of napalm and 3863 rockets. It also fired 396,000 rounds of 0.50-cal ammunition. The results VF-884 achieved with this expended ordnance were also impressive – 2232 enemy troops killed, 842 buildings destroyed and 174 bridges knocked out.

One of VF-884's more memorable missions was flown on 13 May 1951 near the North Korean capital, Pyongyang. This was one of the most heavily defended targets north of the 38th Parallel. The unit was tasked with attacking a busy road complex – which included a bridge – used mainly at night to take supplies to Chinese troops in the frontline. A pilot from the unit described the difficulty of picking out key landmarks on such missions;

'Our carrier usually stayed about 50 miles from the coast, and the first thing we saw on approaching land was the rugged mountainous terrain. Between the ridges were lowlands covered in rice paddies. There were no cities worth mentioning and very few buildings, but plenty of scattered thatched structures. One part of North Korea looked like all the others, and we would navigate inland from a certain point on the coast or follow

a river's course. If we were lucky, we would hook up with a FAC who would direct us to targets.'

As the VF-884 F4Us approached a big bridge, they ran headlong into something they had not expected – heavy fire from multiple large-calibre guns. Lt Cdr Glen Carmichael led his division of four Corsairs into the incoming fire, as their assigned task was flak suppression. Lt Garrison and his division were carrying the 1000-lb GP bombs intended to destroy the bridge. One of the Corsairs scored a direct hit, which dropped a span. Another bomb hit the railway line leading to the

bridge, twisting the steel rails and scattering sleepers all over the area. It was a successful mission, as there had been no losses among the attacking pilots. Their F4Us returned with plenty of bullet holes, however.

Five days later, however, Lt Garrison was shot down and listed as missing in action, while Lt Dragastin, who had scored a direct hit on the bridge, was killed while providing cover for the downed Garrison. The squadron also subsequently lost its CO, Lt Cdr Glen Carmichael, who was listed as killed in action.

Aside from its two F4U units, CVG-101 also boasted a Reserve-manned AD-2/4Q unit (VA-702 from NAS Dallas, Texas) and F9F-2B squadron (VF-721 from NAS Glenview, Illinois). During this deployment, the air group logged a total of 8567 sorties, which equated to 23,627 flying hours. The so-called 'weekend warriors' had made a significant contribution to the US Navy's war effort.

OFFENSIVE BUSTING

During early July 1951, the Eighth Army carefully monitored Chinese movements just north of the bomb line. Intelligence determined that the communists were stockpiling 800 tons of food and supplies per day, which could mean only one thing – they were planning a major attack.

After a successful close air support mission on 22 June 1951, this F4U-4 from VF-884 makes the long flight back to *Boxer*. Its pilot on this occasion was Lt Warren Mayhugh (*Bill Wallace*)

Two US Navy F4U-4s are serviced and refuelled at a small airfield in South Korea before returning to *Boxer*. The Corsair in the foreground was assigned to VF-884 and the fighter behind it to VF-791. Both aircraft are still fully armed, suggesting that bad weather or mechanical problems may have forced them to land ashore (*Bill Wallace*)

One of the most active carrier air groups in the war was CVG-2. This photograph was taken when the group was embarked in *Philippine Sea* during the second of the vessel's four combat cruises, which ran from March to June 1951 – it was CVG-2's third deployment to Korea. F4U-4s of VF-24, VF-63 and VF-64 can be seen at the aft end of the flightdeck (*Tailhook Association*)

It was also clear that if this situation was not handled promptly, UN ground forces might be facing an offensive of unparalleled ferocity.

On 6 July, Gen Matthew Ridgway informed the Joint Chiefs of Staff of Intelligence reports indicating that the Chinese were preparing for an all-out offensive. To prevent this, plans were drawn up for a large-scale interdiction campaign against north-south rail traffic. This would include a maximum effort against all railway bridges to immobilise the enemy's heavy repair equipment that depended on rail transport for movement. As this was too much for the eight USAF wings based in South Korea to achieve, the US Navy was asked to provide help with its carrier-borne aircraft. Missions would begin on 18 August and, with five carriers on station, their air groups would clearly play a major role.

Corsair units contributed heavily by attacking rail targets deep inside North Korea. *Essex, Boxer, Bon Homme Richard, Princeton* and *Sicily* all provided F4U, F9F and AD aircraft. Despite the Corsair units flying countless missions, official records for mid-August reveal that no F4Us were lost by the US Navy and Marine Corps squadrons involved.

Sadly, this was more an exception to the rule, however, as by 5 October 1951, the US Navy alone had lost 125 Corsairs in combat or to operational causes. But the effective work done by the low-flying World War 2 propeller-driven types was having a devastating effect on enemy ground troops. Combined with the missions flown by the various UN jet types, these attacks were making it impossible for the Chinese and North Koreans to move anything by road and rail during daylight hours. Traffic heading for the frontlines was therefore forced to move at night. But even that was no guarantee of safety because the F4U-5Ns, Marine F7F-3N Tigercats and USAF B-26 Invaders were on patrol most nights.

On very rare occasions the communists still risked moving troops during daylight hours. Lt John White of Reserve-manned VF-791, embarked in *Boxer*, was witness to one such event during a sortie over North Korea in September 1951;

'This mission has always puzzled me. We were hunting for targets between Hamhung and Hungnam, and I was in a flight of four Corsairs. As luck would have it, there was a levee alongside a river, and as we passed over it we noticed a large group of Chinese soldiers marching four abreast in a column some 100 yards long! They seemed to be completely oblivious to the four F4Us overhead. Perhaps they were bluffing, or they thought we hadn't seen them.

'Anyway, after a short radio discussion between the four of us, we clicked on all 0.50-cal guns and started strafing the column. The soldiers immediately broke ranks and ran for the ditches on both sides of the levee,

Lt Jack Bucknum was a high-time veteran of VF-63. His squadron was part of CVG-2, which had an outstanding Korean War record of four cruises aboard three different carriers. Note the gold 'football' helmet as worn by most Navy pilots during this period. The squadron's aircraft displayed the tail code 'M' (*Grant Bucknum*)

VF-791 pilot Lt John White straps in with the help of his plane captain, ADE3 Felix Norris. Note the Confederate flag worn on the right shoulder by squadron pilots – the unit's nickname was the 'Rebels', and its home base prior to mobilisation was NAS Memphis, Tennessee (*Felix Norris*)

but it was too late. We had clear shots at all of them as they were very exposed. The body count after we finished our runs was very high. We never understood why they were so brazen as to show themselves as if nothing was around to cause them harm. More than likely, they were reinforcements heading for the frontline. This mission, like most we flew, lasted between three and three-and-a-half hours.'

VF-791 was paired with VF-884 during this deployment, these units being the first Naval Air Reserve-manned F4U squadrons to see combat in Korea. VF-791 chalked up some amazing statistics on that cruise, tallying 1250 sorties and 3600 flying hours. Its pilots (who logged at least 60 missions each) expended 750,000 lbs of bombs and five-inch rockets in destroying 175 bridges, 140 trucks, 20 supply dumps, 125 rail cars and more than 500 miscellaneous buildings.

The success of many thousands of combat sorties flown by US Navy and Marine Corsair pilots cannot be put down to the skill or good luck of the pilots involved. Without the dedicated enlisted maintenance and ordnance personnel these squadrons would not have been able to report such impressive achievements. Their work days were long, and for those on the ground conditions were often difficult. Serving below deck on the carriers during hot summers and bitterly cold winters was no picnic either, whilst working on a narrow flightdeck with 30+ propellers turning was dangerous enough even when the weather was good.

US Navy Aviation Electronicsman Second Class Leon Bryant served aboard *Bon Homme Richard* with VF-874, which was part of CVG-102 during the vessel's May-December 1951 combat cruise. Here, he recalls some of the hazardous jobs the unsung flightdeck crewmen had to perform in all weathers in order to keep the F4Us in the war;

'I helped the pilots before take-off with their radio problems and interviewed them when they returned from missions to see if they had encountered any in-flight maladies. I was on the flightdeck during most operations, day and night, and witnessed most of the accidents that occurred there. I spent countless hours in the cockpits of the F4Us doing radio checks and repairs.

'I also rode the brakes when they were moving aircraft around on the deck, which was very scary. When "re-spotting the deck", the technique was to hook a tow-bar to

This VF-791 Corsair works with
a FAC as it prepares for a strafing
run on enemy positions close to
the frontlines in central Korea
(*Tailhook Association*)

the aircraft, tow it behind a tractor "mule" to get the aeroplane rolling fast enough to travel on its own and then steer it with the brakes. If there was someone in the cockpit working on the aircraft at the time, he was expected to steer it when the tractor driver released the tow bar. Sometimes, they wanted the aircraft in one of the corners, with its tailwheel within feet of the end of the flightdeck. You would roll rapidly toward the fantail, and at the appointed place hit one of the brake pedals and hopefully turn the Corsair through 180 degrees. The secret was not to panic and drive the aircraft off the edge of the fantail.

'The forward visibility from the F4U's cockpit was extremely poor, and it was even worse when there was no parachute pack to sit on. When manoeuvring the aircraft, it was necessary to rely on hand signals from someone standing beside it. At night, re-spotting was even more dangerous because hand signals were replaced by a waving torch.

'The flightdeck was made of steel, covered with about one-and-a-half inches of Douglas fir planking. After several months of operations, the wooden deck became saturated with oil dripping from all those R-2800 engines, making it very slippery. Moving among the aircraft on deck with all the engines running was, to say the least, very hazardous. We were told that if we fell, we were to spread eagle and not attempt to get up. An F4U could taxi over you if you were lying prone, but that 14ft four-bladed prop might get you if you stuck your butt up too far! You could also catch the jet blast from one of the F9F Panthers taxiing toward the catapult.

'The slippery deck meant that we lost a lot of tail cones chewed off by the guy in the aircraft behind. Even with the brakes full on, the tyres would creep forward a few inches while sliding on the slippery deck. It was especially treacherous after light rain.

'The wooden deck also shed splinters. The prop blast would blow slivers into your skin like you wouldn't believe. We wore helmets and goggles to protect our faces and eyes. Slamming a Corsair cockpit canopy shut was also dangerous, and more than one crewman lost a finger. But the thing topside personnel feared most was an arresting cable parting. Sometimes they had to change a cable or two every couple of days if operations were frequent. There were 13 cross-deck pennants, as they were called, and if the pilot was lucky, he caught one of the first three or four cables. But those aft cables took a beating, and if one broke under tension, watch out! Fortunately, I never saw that happen.'

VF-874's sister-squadron in CVG-102 was VF-783. One of the unit's pilots was Lt(jg) Walter Spangenberg, who flew a mission in late November 1951 that saw his division attacking targets in a sector known as 'Baker-Uncle' in the landlocked north-central area of North Korea. Operations in this region were considered to be particularly hazardous because it was hundreds of miles from the coast, thus reducing a downed pilot's chances of being rescued by helicopter. Spangenberg recalled;

'The strike was against railway and highway bridges that crossed a river valley between high mountains. These bridges were defended by a significant number of AAA batteries sited on high ground on both sides of the valley. Assigned to take these targets out were four AD-3s from VA-923 and four F4Us from my squadron. Normally, we would have used our F9Fs for flak suppression, but the target was way beyond their range.

'In order to have a greater chance of success, we would dive along the length of the bridges and then release our ordnance, thus ensuring that any bombs that fell short or long would have a chance of hitting the target. The enemy gunners knew this, of course, and had arranged their batteries accordingly. The strike was well carried out, with the fighters diving first on the flak positions, followed by the AD-3s, with their larger bombs, on the bridges. We scored several good hits and suffered no losses as we joined up for the long flight back to the carrier.'

As the aircraft left the area in loose formation, the fighter-bombers were suddenly attacked by two MiG-15s. The Soviet fighters had been spotted seconds earlier by one of the F4U pilots, who had warned the others, but few had heard him due to deficiencies with the newly installed ARC-27 UHF radio equipment. The flight scattered like buckshot, with only a few pilots realising what was happening. The MiGs made one firing pass, hitting a Skyraider, before heading back north. Had they stayed, their pilots would have enjoyed easy pickings, but their fuel was probably running low. The flight regrouped around the stricken AD, which was now trailing smoke, and headed for Wonsan Harbour, where a US Navy helicopter could retrieve its pilot if he had to ditch or bale out.

The Skyraider had suffered serious damage, which was to be expected considering the MiG-15 was armed with 23 mm and 37 mm cannons. As the formation worked its way towards the coast, the AD steadily lost altitude, but its pilot was able to reach Wonsan. He baled out into a cold and windswept November sea. Division lead had organised a rescue flight for the downed pilot, but as the surviving strike aircraft were running low on fuel and still had to recover aboard the carrier, a further call was made for back up to support the rescue helicopter. Diverting to a land base in South Korea was out of the question because the distance to the carrier was considerably shorter. Lt(jg) Spangenberg takes up the story;

'A relief flight arrived, and the remaining aircraft from the original strike force departed for *Bon Homme Richard's* assumed position. The carrier, in the meantime, had heard of the MiG attack by radio and abandoned its position. The ship had sailed eastwards, assuming a condition of radio silence for everything except the low frequency YE coded beacon. All this caused some anxiety among the strike group's pilots, but we found the carrier heading east and stayed in the air long

F4U-4s of CVG-15's VF-713 prepare to receive their ordnance for the next strike mission to be flown from USS *Antietam* (CV-36) during the carrier's sole Korean War cruise in 1951-52. The squadron's Corsairs displayed the tail code 'H'. VF-713 also made just one combat deployment (*Tailhook Association*)

enough for it to turn into the wind. All of us got aboard, despite 50 knots of wind blowing over the deck on a very windy afternoon. We found out that our AD pilot had been rescued and was on his way back to the ship. It was an eventful mission that will long be remembered.'

By late 1951, the most attractive targets in North Korea such as the bridges attacked by CVG-102 were located in the Pyongyang area and further north near the Yalu River. Going after these targets placed the attacking aircraft well within reach of MiG-15s based in Manchuria. During Lt(jg) Spangenberg's cruise, aircraft from his air group were constantly attacking targets protected by intense AAA and, potentially, MiGs. His squadronmate Lt(jg) Pete Colapietro described one such mission when he was flying in a mixed division as 'tail-end Charlie';

'In addition to the missions we normally flew overland, we occasionally undertook anti-submarine patrols. I had also completed the Naval Gunfire Spotting course just prior to our departure from San Diego, and this qualified me to carry out spotting for our battleships off the coast of North Korea. I don't recall exactly which one I worked with, but I think it was USS *Missouri* (BB-63). It shelled the hell out of Wonsan, but the gunners never managed to hit the tall smoke stacks that were my primary target for the ship!

'The more dangerous moments that my squadron faced on cruise came during the dive-bombing and strafing of heavily defended target areas up north. During the final week of our cruise, I was launched as a standby pilot. Upon joining up, I discovered to my surprise that I was to be a "tail-end Charlie" on a flight of two divisions of AD-4s. That meant there would be seven Skyraiders and one Corsair in the strike force.

'Those aircraft could carry the bomb load of a World War 2-era B-17, absorb plenty of punishment and still return home. Our F4Us, however, had to carry a drop tank of fuel in order to match the range of the AD-4. That limited us to a single 1000-lb bomb, or two 500 "pounders", and/or rockets. On this particular mission we were attacking the primary north-south railway line, and after three runs I was out of ordnance except for my 0.50-cal rounds. The ADs continued on run after run, dropping all their "good stuff", and I followed them down just strafing, hoping to do some good in taking out enemy gun positions.

'Once out of ammo and bombs, our two divisions formed up for the return to the carrier, flying in a loose formation. Approaching the coast, I saw half a dozen tracers pass by my Corsair. Seconds later, I realised that we were under attack from the air, and I radioed a warning to the rest of the formation. I then made a sharp right turn and flipped on my master armament switch, hoping that I still had some ammunition left. But it was too late, for the two MiG-15s were already well out of range.'

The communist fighters had spotted the division and decided on a hit-and-run attack on the tail-end Corsair. Fortunately for Colapietro, the MiG pilots' aim was a little off and the rounds passed harmlessly over his canopy. One of the AD-3s was hit, however, although its pilot was able to return safely to the carrier. It was a close call at the conclusion of a successful mission that had inflicted considerable damage on the north-south railway line.

INCREASED INTERDICTION

In its mission planning, Far East Air Force (FEAF), which controlled all USAF assets in-theatre, placed strong emphasis on halting the movement of Chinese troops and materiel from Manchuria to the frontlines. UN aircraft exacted a heavy toll on road and rail traffic accordingly as part of Operation *Strangle*, but supplies still got though nevertheless. By late 1951, there was concern in-theatre that the enemy might be on the verge of accumulating enough ammunition and other equipment to mount an effective offensive in the early spring of 1952. It was therefore decided to escalate *Strangle* by dovetailing TF 77's assets into the operation.

The first attacks undertaken by naval aircraft commenced on 28 December, and TF 77's commitment to this intense offensive ran through to 1 February 1952. Corsairs, Panthers and Skyraiders participated in the strikes, which resulted in the breaching of 2782 railway lines, the destruction of 79 railway bridges and 50 other vital targets. This undermined the enemy's attempts to stockpile supplies near the frontlines, and it also overloaded the previously effective repair organisation. Intelligence photos showed that in many places where damage had been extensive, repair crews were unable to renew broken lines for up to ten days. In the past, such damage had been fixed within hours.

One of the units heavily involved in this campaign was VF-653, which was the solitary Reserve-manned unit embarked in *Valley Forge* with Air

VF-653 worked-up over Hawaii in October 1951 as preparation for the unit's sole combat cruise, embarked in *Valley Forge*. This photograph was taken just prior to the ship sailing for Korea. Piloting the Corsair is Lt Robert Sobey, who was subsequently killed in action on 22 December 1951 when his F4U-4 BuNo 81946 was hit by AAA and crashed just east of Yonghung (*Bob Balser*)

Task Group 1 during CV-45's third war cruise (from October 1951 to July 1952). The sole F4U-4B-equipped attack unit aboard the carrier, it suffered its fair share of casualties during eight months of combat.

As previously mentioned, more than 500 Corsairs were lost during the Korean War, but most of the pilots involved were plucked from hostile territory, or the sea, by rescue helicopters. One of the most hazardous rescue operations undertaken during the campaign involved Ens Ed Sterrett of VF-653. This event, which took place on 26 May 1952, is recalled by squadronmate Lt Bob Balser;

'I was leading a flight of four F4Us against a target deep in North Korea. We peeled off into trail formation so that each pilot could concentrate totally on the target. As I pulled out of my dive, I immediately banked sharply to the right to observe our bombs hit, and to also keep track of the other three aircraft. When I got them in view I was shocked to see one of our F4Us spinning toward the ground. I yelled "Bale Out!", but my wingman, Ed Sterrett, was already floating down in his parachute. I immediately called *Valley Forge* and rescue procedures were started.

'The terrain was over 6000 ft above sea level, so when the chopper arrived the thin air wouldn't allow it to hover. It made several passes over the wooded area to try and get to Ed, but it was impossible. As we were running low on fuel, we had to return to the carrier. That night, the task force steamed south to get close to a Marine airfield, where we could embark two of their big HRS-2 helicopters with their three-man crews. The next day, we returned to the area with the two choppers to search for our downed pilot. Two of our F4Us circled at 1000 ft while my wingman, "Rollo" Bush, and I went much lower. Since it was a planned search, our aircraft were fitted with two belly tanks to give us much more loiter time.'

'Rollo' Bush's aircraft, flying at treetop height, was hit by ground fire. He had pulled contrails trying to avoid it, but he was unsuccessful. There was a spectacular fireball as the two belly tanks exploded and the aircraft crashed. Balser and the two remaining pilots circled in the hope of spotting Bush. One of the naval aviators thought that he had seen a man a short distance from the crash site, but the others could hardly believe it was 'Rollo'. Amazingly, he turned up as a released prisoner at the end of the war. Balser resumes the story;

'In the meantime, the Marine helicopters arrived, and one was immediately despatched to the site. As it tried to hover in the thin air, it too crashed. Its three-man crew were unhurt, and the next day another Marine helicopter was sent in to pick them up. Having by now realised the inability of their helo to hover at such high altitudes, the crew decided to use a rope ladder and pick up each individual "on the run".

'I participated in all of these flights, circling above the helo and occasionally firing off a few rounds to discourage enemy forces from trying to interfere. When the HRS-2 made its first pass, the co-pilot grabbed the ladder and slowly climbed up. As he did so, the helo swung out over a deep valley, thousands of feet above the ground. It was like watching a circus act, and I had a front row seat! The second time around, a sergeant caught the ladder and proceeded to climb up, but he only got half way and stopped. They flew around for the final pass and picked up the pilot.

'Later, at the debriefing, the sergeant explained that he was so terrified when they swung out over the valley that he couldn't move. He then realised that he had to make room for the pilot, so he climbed up a few rungs. On the last pass he was afraid to look down, but he felt a jolt on the rope ladder and assumed that the pilot was aboard. Having finally got the courage to look down and be sure, he stated, "I saw the pilot, who had his legs hooked through the rungs of the ladder, thus leaving his hands free to take pictures with his camera!" From that point the sergeant had no trouble in climbing the rest of the way up!

'By then both Ed Sterrett and "Rollo" Bush had been captured, and they were PoWs for more than a year. After release, "Rollo" was being checked out in various jet types in order to be a Landing Signal Officer. He experienced a "cold cat-shot" (catapult failure), his aircraft fell off the bow and he was never recovered. Sterrett was a flight instructor in the training command. He experienced a mid-air collision and survived another bale out. Before his capture, Sterrett had ditched a Corsair in the Sea of Japan after it had received heavy flak damage.'

PRINCETON AND CVG-19

Princeton, having missed out on combat in World War 2 (it was commissioned in November 1945), would see more than its fair share of action during the Korean War. Between November 1950 and September 1953, the vessel undertook four combat cruises off the North Korean coast. On two of these deployments the vessel embarked CVG-19, which of course included two squadrons of F4Us within its ranks.

One of those units was VF-192, which saw action from CV-37 during its first war cruise in 1950-51 and then again during its third in 1952. Amongst the pilots serving with the squadron during the latter deployment was Lt George W Nichols, who not only flew day missions but also became experienced in night intruder work, despite his F4U-4 lacking a radar. He explained;

'Having deployed on 21 March 1952, we stopped in Hawaii for a brief stay while we got ready for combat. We easily passed the operational readiness inspection, as CVG-19 and the ship worked very well together.

'Our first assignments involved stopping the flow of supplies from China to the frontline in central Korea. During the day, we would drop bombs on communist railway lines and bridges, and during the night they would repair everything. They had supply dumps just north of the Yalu River, and they would mass everything within that safe zone. As soon as it was dark, the Chinese would start moving supplies south out of Manchuria – we were strictly forbidden from bombing anything in Chinese territory. With all this traffic moving at night, the only unit in CVG-19 getting any action during the early evening hours was VC-3 Det E, equipped with a handful of F4U-5N nightfighters.

'Our squadron CO, Lt Cdr "Ace" Parker, realised this, and fortunately for him, he had deliberately filled VF-192 with highly trained pilots proficient in instrument flying. Even though we were a day Corsair squadron, we had the capability to do significant damage to the enemy at night. "Ace" finally talked Seventh Fleet into letting us try, but there was a catch. We had to fly our assigned day missions too, and not use the night operations as an excuse to miss our scheduled sorties.

'I was one of five pilots who volunteered to fly the night interdiction plan, with "Ace" making the sixth. When we got started, we did as much, or more, damage to truck and rail movements than the rest of air group combined during the day. The reason for this was that virtually everything was moving at night.

'The drill for those pilots selected to fly at night was to catapult from *Princeton* at 0400 hrs and return just after sunrise. We would have breakfast and then attend the briefing for the day's missions. There was time for rest, but flying had priority.

'Night missions certainly had their rewards too. When you hit a truck filled with ammunition it was like the 4th of July, with all the fireworks. When you hit a locomotive, the sparks and steam could be seen for miles, even on a moonless night. Also, when the enemy shot at us, we knew exactly where the guns were located, and could quickly retaliate with rockets or 0.50-cal rounds. We were also getting more than our share of commendations. Seventh Fleet finally decided that we were getting too good, and it made us stop the night intruder missions.'

The standard operating procedure for CVG-19 during that cruise was to use the F9F Panthers of VF-191 for ground fire suppression and the Corsairs (of VF-192 and VF-193) for light dive-bombing and strafing. The AD-4 Skyraiders of VA-195 acted as heavy bombers, and they were able to destroy major targets such as bridges, railway tunnels and underground bunkers. Lt Nichols explained;

'Before an attack began, it was normal to mill around until everyone was in parade formation. Enemy gunners were therefore alerted before any attack, and they knew that the ADs packed the biggest punch, so they usually held their fire until the Skyraiders approached. Routinely, the communist gunners would attempt to shoot the ADs down before they could release their ordnance.

'It was against regulations to attack any village without Seventh Fleet approval. The enemy was aware of this, so they concentrated their AAA in the villages. One such village was well known to CVG-19, for it was the location of a radar-equipped AAA site. It had given the game away by firing at us on cloudy days as we flew overhead to a nearby target. By revealing their location, the gunners actually helped us to navigate around the village in future – from then on we would have it well marked on our target maps.

'Eventually, Seventh Fleet decided that those gun emplacements had to go regardless of the policy of sparing villages. When we launched the resulting strike, the leader's radio became unserviceable so I took over. I radioed the F9Fs, as they had been the last to launch and had not yet caught up, and I also told the AD force that there would be no circling the target until all the attackers were in place. When we arrived overhead the village, the F4Us and ADs initiated their attack, and we were back on the carrier just 30 minutes after taking off. The gun batteries were totally destroyed in what was acknowledged to be one of CVG-19's smoothest attacks of the entire war.'

VF-192 flew the F4U-4 during both of its Korean War deployments with CVG-19 aboard *Princeton*. The squadron's aircraft displayed the tail code 'B' during both cruises (*Tailhook Association*)

Later in his tour, Lt Nichols was shot down, but he managed to ditch in the sea and was rescued by a helicopter from the battleship USS *Iowa* (BB-61).

HYDROELECTRIC PLANTS

Most of the power for North Korea and southern Manchuria was produced by hydroelectric powerplants sited near the Yalu River – the largest of these was the Sui-ho plant. To say that these choice targets were well defended would be an understatement. As well as there being literally hundreds of AAA batteries in the immediate vicinity of the plants, the major MiG-15 bases were just minutes away north of the Yalu.

In May 1952 the peace talks at Panmunjom, which had started a year earlier, became bogged down. The UN decided that to encourage progress the hydroelectric plants should be targeted for the first time. It took about a month to plan a massive, well-coordinated attack, which was carried out on the afternoon of 23 June in one of the war's biggest strikes. All of the carriers operating in the combat zone contributed aircraft, and there were large forces from the Marines Corps and USAF too. Indeed, the latter put up more than 100 F-86 Sabres to protect the fighter-bombers from being targeted by MiG-15s.

Six aircraft carriers were in-theatre at the time – *Boxer*, *Valley Forge*, *Philippine Sea*, *Princeton*, *Bon Homme Richard* and *Essex*, the latter having just come on station. This meant that eight US Navy Corsair squadrons were available, although not all were needed. All Panther and Skyraider units embarked in these vessels did participate, however. As intended, the strike influenced the peace talks.

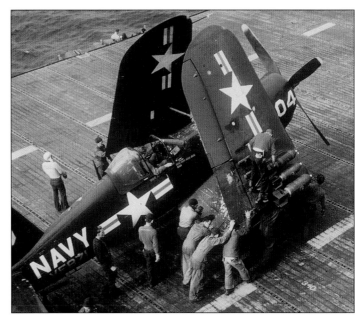

VF-871 also completed two Korean War deployments. This photograph was taken on the deck of *Essex* during its second cruise, as part of ATG-2, in 1952-53. VF-871 was the only F4U squadron embarked, although there was a small detachment of F4U-5N nightfighter Corsairs from VC-3 Det I aboard too (*National Archives*)

These hardworking maintenance personnel were assigned to VF-64 aboard *Boxer* during the spring of 1952 (*G D Kovener*)

The F4U squadrons' groundcrew represented the key factor in keeping the serviceability rate high during the war. Pictured aboard *Valley Forge* during its 1952 cruise are maintenance personnel of VF-92 – the ship's only Corsair day squadron on this deployment (*Ed Ellstrom*)

Marked up with a unit badge and bomb tally beneath the windscreen, a well-weathered F4U-4 of VF-113 taxies along the flightdeck of *Philippine Sea* prior to taking off in the late spring of 1952. All the primary squadrons of CVG-11 displayed the letter 'V' on their vertical stabilisers (*'Ace' Jewell*)

Naval records show that only F4U-4 BuNo 81299 was lost, this aircraft being flown by VF-63's CO, Lt Cdr Ward Miller. The Corsair was hit by AAA south of Tanchon, but Miller managed to reach the coast and bale out – he was quickly rescued by a US Navy helicopter. VF-63 was operating from *Boxer*, and Miller's aircraft was the 204th US Navy F4U to be lost in the war.

Ens D W 'Ace' Jewell was a VF-113 pilot flying from *Philippine Sea* with CVG-11 during this period. His squadron was usually assigned some of the toughest targets, so the dam and hydroelectric plant that they were assigned on 23 June did not faze them. Jewell has a clear recollection of that mission, despite it having occurred almost 60 years ago;

'The launch went off without a hitch and the strike force joined up quickly as we proceeded toward the beach. VF-113 was to rendezvous with our Skyraider unit, VA-115, near the target before we began the assault. Our squadron of Corsairs consisted of 14 aircraft out of a possible 16. We had three divisions of four aircraft and one section of two aircraft. I was flying wing in the two-ship, so I was "tail-end Charlie". The weather was fair, with scattered cumulus clouds. We tightened up our formation when we crossed the coastline as our target was up on the Yalu.

'As we approached the target, the clouds began to build, making the hydroelectric plant difficult to identify. We were flying low, trying to get onto the right track, when we encountered a dead-end in a valley. The entire squadron had to climb up into the clouds and then go back down into the next valley. I was too busy staying in tight formation with my leader to figure out where we were. Finally, we were close enough to see the reservoir in the distance.

'At that point we established contact with the Skyraiders and, while waiting for them, my squadron widened its circle around the target.

'Across the Yalu was a communist airfield and, so help me, there were a lot of MiG-15s practicing touch-and-go landings! Now my head was really on a swivel, because I knew we were going to be jumped by some of them. We probably circled for 15 minutes or more, and my thoughts were that we were sure giving them plenty of time to get ready for us! The big moment finally came, and all our aircraft moved towards the dam. There was still no flak as we all got into position. Since the gun emplacements we had been told to knock out were silent, my leader was hastily directed to hit a building that

Mission complete and safely back aboard the 'Phil Sea', the pilot of this VF-113 F4U-4 has already activated the fighter's wing folding mechanism as he trundles towards the bow of *Philippine Sea* during the 1951-52 cruise. Note that all the Corsair's ordnance has been expended during the sortie (*'Ace' Jewell*)

US Navy Corsair pilots had a choice of headwear, namely a hard helmet or a leather one. These VF-113 pilots are wearing a variety of headgear as they prepare for a strike from *Philippine Sea*. At far left is Ens 'Ace' Jewell (*'Ace' Jewell*)

was the powerplant office, or so it appeared.

'At last we started our bombing dives, and at that moment the crap hit the fan as we came down. I was stepped down on my leader and had all the switches positioned when the flak balls started up at us. Let me tell you, it keeps one busy trying to fly wing and get the pipper on the gunsight where you want it.

'We had orders to expend all of our ordnance, so why not salvo all of the rockets and bombs at once? That's exactly what I did, amid all the yelling and noise coming over the radio. Squeezing off short bursts of my 20 mm as I followed the leader in a dive, as he dropped, I salvoed all of my ordnance.

'In the meantime, guys were calling out who was hit by flak and departing the area. Pulling out and starting a circle, you could see that the ADs of VA-115 had done a magnificent job on the face of the dam. Bomb hits in the "Comstock" area caused the water to spurt hundreds of feet into the air.'

The Corsairs pulled out of their dives low and at full throttle, leaving the flak and smoke far behind them. Ens Jewell's flight had scored direct hits, levelling the building. The heavily loaded Skyraiders were right behind the F4Us, and they needed more altitude for their release. This meant that the AAA was concentrating on them, and Jewell's flight had to weave through the fire as they attempted to clear the target area;

'We were manoeuvring sharply so as to avoid as much of the AAA as we could, and for a brief moment we were caught in the middle of the crossfire. With the speed generated and the low pull-out, we were going through the hail of lead from gun pits on the ridge lines to our right and left. It didn't seem to matter to the gunners that their weapons were shooting at each other while they were trying to nail us.

'As we attempted to gain altitude and head for the coast, our radios were jammed with chatter about damage caused by AAA. Many of the attacking aircraft were streaming hydraulic fluid, and pilots were reporting various other failures. The guard channel was now like an old-fashioned party line, with a cacophony of sound. But none of the Corsairs in CVG-11 received damage serious enough to warrant their pilots baling out or ditching.

'I landed safely back aboard *Philippine Sea*, and as I taxied to the

This F4U-4 from VF-74 is heading back to *Bon Homme Richard* after a strike on North Korea. This unit (participating in its sole war deployment) was the only Corsair day squadron operating with CVG-7 during the 'Bonnie Dick's' 1952-53 cruise (*Tailhook Association*)

VF-152 pilot Lt Edward 'Buzz' Purcell had an eventful combat tour in 1953, being shot down on 3 May and fished out of the sea, and then suffering serious wounds to his left arm when his fighter was left badly holed by heavy AAA a few weeks later. Applying a tourniquet to his arm, Purcell then managed to land his crippled Corsair at an airfield in South Korea. He is seen here standing beside his bullet-riddled aircraft shortly after completing this hair-raising mission (*E B 'Buzz' Purcell*)

parking area, I gave a thumbs up to the maintenance chief, who immediately gave me a distinct thumbs down. This meant that I was to taxi to the elevator for the ride down to the hangar deck.

'As I was exiting the cockpit I noticed a number of maintenance crew members pointing all over my aircraft. I soon found out why – they found 162 holes in my F4U, but none of the rounds had hit anything vital. To this day I've never figured out how they counted all those holes. Anyway, it sure took a lot of patches to get that old bird ready to fly again.'

In the wake of these well executed raids on the various hydroelectric plants, and their dams, the communists significantly boosted the AAA defences protecting the few key targets that remained intact in North Korea. Intelligence determined that during the winter of 1952-53, approximately 786 large-calibre guns and more than 1600 automatic weapons had been installed to discourage further strikes.

The main weapon in this enhanced arsenal was the Soviet-built M-1939 85 mm gun, which had an effective ceiling of 25,000 ft. The smaller M-1939 37 mm cannon could fire 160 rounds a minute up to 4500 ft, and this was the weapon most feared by pilots of low-flying F4Us and F-51s. Both 37 mm and 85 mm guns now ringed targets such as Pyongyang, Sui-ho, the Sinanju bridges and Antung airfield.

The guns sited in what the Americans called 'MiG Alley' did not pose a threat to the slower fighter-bombers because targets in this area were assigned to the faster F-84 Thunderjets and, later, F-86F fighter-bombers, which would arrive in early 1953. Corsair pilots concentrated on interrupting supply lines and supporting the troops.

PRINCETON's FINAL WAR CRUISE

Princeton's final combat cruise was undertaken between 24 January and 21 September 1953, with CVG-15 embarked. By this last stage in the war, only a single Corsair attack squadron was included within the air group's ranks, namely VF-152. A handful of F4U-5Ns from VC-3 Det D were also embarked. Two squadrons of Panthers (VF-153 and VF-154) and one of Skyraiders (VA-155) provided the bulk of CVG-15's 'punch'.

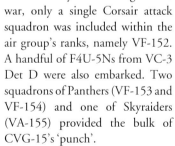

On 3 May the air group was tasked with attacking targets close to the frontlines. Lt Edward 'Buzz' Purcell was in a flight of Corsairs targeting Chinese supply dumps when his engine was hit by AAA. As the shell exploded, he saw a huge

orange fireball envelope the nose of his F4U, closely followed by flames pouring out from beneath the engine cowling. He recalled what happened next;

'After 15 or 20 seconds the fire went out, at which point the propeller stopped turning. I remember reading "Hamilton" in bright yellow letters on the frozen prop! It became very quiet as my Corsair turned into a glider. Fortunately for me, I wasn't too far inland from the coast, and I was able to glide to the ocean, where I ditched about half-a-mile from shore.

'The aircraft's forward motion caused it to plunge straight in beneath the waves. In seconds it was totally submerged, and it was then that I remembered my training in the "Dilbert Dunker" at NAS Pensacola. Reaching the surface, I unbuckled my parachute and was about to inflate my life raft when I heard the distinct sound of automatic weapons fire from the nearby beach.

'I immediately gave up on the brightly coloured life raft and decided to depend on my "Mae West" to move out of range of the soldiers on the shore. I didn't inflate it right away, as I relied on my "poopy suit" to help me float out of the way. In a very short time, a flight of Corsairs arrived overhead, and they made several strafing runs on the enemy forces firing at me. They silenced the hostile guns and then left to return to *Princeton*.

'It then became very quiet, so I inflated my raft. About half-an-hour later a helicopter arrived overhead. The crew lowered a sling, pulled me up and took me to an LST, after which I was transferred to a cruiser and from there back to my carrier. Having returned to *Princeton*, I was saddened to hear that two of my fellow pilots from VF-152 had been lost due to the accurate AAA over the target that day. I was very lucky because a number of the rescue efforts to pick up downed pilots in the sea off North Korea didn't go as well as mine.'

Essex **undertook two cruises during the Korean War. On its second, in 1952-53, VF-871 was the only Corsair day squadron embarked. This aircraft is seen shortly after extricating itself from the arresting cables at mission-end, the pilot already beginning to fold the fighter's wings (***Bruce Bagwell***)**

The new exposure or 'poopy' suits saved the lives of several pilots when they had to ditch in frigid waters off North Korea. These VF-152 Corsair pilots are seen testing their newly issued suits in cold Japanese waters prior to heading back into combat aboard *Princeton* in early 1953 (*E B 'Buzz' Purcell*)

By the time *Princeton* began its final war cruise in early 1953, US Navy ships were now more concerned with minesweeping and conducting surface and aerial patrols in the Yellow Sea, Sea of Japan and the Korean Straits. The number of air strikes mounted by the carrier force had steadily dwindled as the war progressed due to a paucity of targets in North Korea. The Chinese were restricting movement to the hours of darkness, shifting the attack burden to B-26 Invader crews, as well as US Navy and Marine Corps F4U-5N units.

Despite a slackening in the mission tempo for F4U units leading up to the cessation of fighting in Korea on 27 July 1953, during the war's final 12 months, Corsair units of the US Navy and Marine Corps had lost 170 aircraft to AAA. Overall, for the entire 37-month war, the US Navy lost 722 aircraft (including 389 F4Us) to all causes, of which 358 were to enemy action. Most of these aircraft fell victim to AAA. Effectively, a carrier air group could expect to lose ten percent of its aircrew during a deployment – this figure remained constant for the duration of the Korean War.

Yet despite these overwhelming losses, carrier-based units had logged some impressive achievements. Of the 27 participating F4U squadrons, many had completed multiple deployments. Of these, VF-63 and VF-64 had undertaken four separate cruises, while VF-24 logged three. Nine other squadrons each recorded two tours.

The final mission tally for all US Navy aircraft totalled 255,545 combat sorties, during which 163,062 tons of bombs were dropped and 267,217 rockets fired. Records also showed that a total of 68,608,000 rounds of ammunition (cannon and machine gun) were fired against enemy targets. US Navy F4U squadrons were major contributors to these impressive statistics.

MARINE CORPS OPERATIONS

The years immediately after World War 2 were hard ones for the US Marine Corps. Funding had been difficult, partly due to the emphasis being placed on equipping the USAF and US Navy with state-of-the-art jets. Although the Marines were at last receiving F9F Panthers, they were not being re-equipped as rapidly as the other services. And when the Korean War began, the shortcomings of the new jets became alarmingly apparent – namely their limited range and inability to operate from crude South Korean airfields.

When the call came, the Marine Corps quickly answered it with MAG-33 and its three F4U Corsair squadrons – day fighter units VMF-214 and VMF-323 and nightfighter squadron VMF(N)-513. Since the situation in South Korea was deteriorating rapidly, it was agreed that both VMF-214 and VMF-323 would operate from light aircraft carriers off the coast. This would free them from using land bases that might be overrun by the enemy or become overcrowded.

VMF-214 'Black Sheep' arrived off the Korean Peninsula aboard USS *Sicily* (CVE-118) on the morning of 3 August 1950 when the war was just six weeks old. At 1630 hrs that same afternoon, the squadron launched its aircraft with full loads of incendiary bombs and rockets. Their targets were heavy troop concentrations in the villages of Chinju and Sinban-ni, where they caught the enemy completely off-guard and inflicted heavy casualties on the North Koreans.

Two Corsairs were also used to shuttle information gathered by USAF reconnaissance aircraft based at Taegu to the carrier, and this intelligence was later used to plan and execute the squadron's next series of missions.

Three days after the 'Black Sheep' began their close air support missions, VMF-323 'Death Rattlers' started flying combat sorties from USS *Badoeng Strait* (CVE-116). Operations commenced on the morning of 6 August and continued without let-up until the final days of the war some 35 months later. The squadron's first sorties were missions against enemy troops using napalm, and they were carried out in conjunction with F-51 Mustangs that were delivering the same ordnance. The body count was very high, and this must have had a significant psychological impact on the surviving North Korean troops in that area.

The use of carriers by Marine Corps Corsairs gave them a distinct advantage when it came to logging a high sortie rate. The USAF Mustangs were wedged tightly into the Pusan perimeter, where it was so crowded that the units operating from there were unable to achieve a 100 per cent serviceability rate. In the meantime, the two Marine squadrons pounded the enemy relentlessly from their carriers, and during August and September the weather was perfect for operations.

At this stage of the war, the North Koreans had yet to pay the heavy price for using the roads and railway lines in daylight that they would in 1951-53. As a result, the fighter-bomber pilots had plenty of targets to choose from. For example, during one August mission flown by VMF-214, a large column of trucks was spotted moving supplies to enemy troops around the perimeter. The first wave of attacking F4Us comprised two divisions with a total of eight aircraft. Within minutes they had destroyed more than 24 trucks. As the attackers headed back to *Sicily*, they left behind numerous smoke columns to indicate the target's location to incoming flights.

During this period, MAG-33's lone Corsair nightfighter squadron, VMF(N)-513, was also flying day missions, as there were few worthwhile targets on offer after dark. That was about to change, however.

On 12 August MAG-12 received orders to move its two Corsair squadrons, VMF-212 and VMF-312, to the Far East – both units were transported to Korea aboard USS *Bataan* (CVL-29). This group also included nightfighter squadron VMF(N)-542, equipped with the F7F-3N Tigercat. Once in-theatre, the units flew in to recently liberated Kimpo AB from Itami AB, in Japan, on 19 September. Once in Korea, orders came through for the groups to swap squadrons. This meant that MAG-12 now controlled the first three units to arrive in-theatre, while the latest arrivals transferred to MAG-33.

The Corsair specialised in low-altitude close air support which made it particularly effective when using 5-in HVAR rockets. This Yonpo-based F4U-4B from VMF-214 has been loaded with the weapons and is ready for another mission in support of the Chosin Reservoir breakout in December 1950 (*Clarence Chick*)

A division of Corsairs from VMF-214 head for the Pusan perimeter from the deck of *Sicily* in the autumn of 1950. The 'Black Sheep' was the first Marine F4U unit to see combat in Korea. Capt John Perrin is flying F4U-4B '16' (*John Perrin*)

INCHON

By this time, the final plans for the amphibious landings at Inchon to relieve the North Korean stranglehold on the Pusan perimeter had been approved. While most USAF fighter-bombers were active in the south, the Marines pounded enemy forces in and around Inchon and Seoul. In its biggest operation since World War 2, the Marine Corps put thousands of men ashore at Inchon on 15 September 1950 in what proved to be a lifesaving move for the UN's efforts to defend the Korean Peninsula. The rapidly moving Marines relied heavily on extensive air support to clear a path for their advance on Seoul. One of the pilots involved in this critical phase of the war was Capt John Perrin of VMF-214;

'Our troops had met some heavy resistance at Yongdungpo, which was an industrial suburb of Seoul. The advance had bogged down due to heavy machine gun fire coming from a metal warehouse. I was flying with my CO, Lt Col Walter Lischeid (who was subsequently killed in action on 25 September 1950), and we had just launched from *Sicily* when we got the call to assist the Marines at Yongdungpo. We were only minutes from the target. I was carrying eight 250-lb frag bombs and a 500-lb VT bomb fused to go off just above the ground. Col Lischeid was carrying only napalm, so I would have to go after the warehouse.

'Working with a FAC, my biggest worry was that our troops were 50 yards from the target, and the possibility of collateral damage was a factor. The building was easy to spot because it was all-metal, as opposed to other structures in the area. I would make my bomb run parallel to the road that separated

The famous 'Death Rattlers' of VMF-323 entered the Korean War with their Corsairs on 6 August 1950, operating from *Badoeng Strait*. Many of the unit's Corsairs displayed a large rattlesnake on their engine cowlings, but such decorations were short-lived, and by mid 1951 VMFA-323 F4Us were soon devoid of identification markings other than the letters 'WS' painted on the vertical stabiliser. This photo was taken at Kimpo (K-14) in the spring of 1951 (*Bill Rockwell*)

Another ferocious looking diamondback rattlesnake is seen on the cowling of this well weathered F4U-4. Photographed in the early summer of 1951, the fighter was embarked in *Sicily* with VMFA-323 at the time (*Conrad Buschmann*)

the target from the friendly troops. This reduced the chances of hitting our guys. I was at 8000 ft when I rolled over and headed down. This was critical because I had to have time to line the target up, and with the fast airspeed that would be increasing, I didn't have much time to locate the warehouse in my sights. As my aircraft was in the vertical, headed down, my speed was approaching 400 knots. It was easy to line up the warehouse, and I waited until my altitude was down to about 2000 ft before releasing the

Fully loaded with 5-in HVARs and a solitary 250-lb bomb, this F4U-4 from VMF-214 is ready to fly its next mission from the deck of the light carrier *Sicily* during the autumn of 1950. The unit was embarked in the vessel from 1 August to 13 November 1950 (*Bill Mitchell*)

500-pounder. You had to stay in the dive long enough to make sure that your bomb was not affected by any G that would throw it off course. When released, it should only have been under the influence of gravity.

'The most dangerous part for the pilot was figuring out when to start pulling up. Your dive speed in a Corsair was very fast, and when you started to pull up you could grey out, which would make it difficult to recover before hitting the ground. In this case, I was able to get the nose up at about 1000 ft, and it took a lot of grunting and concentration to stay alert. As the nose moved above the horizon, I poured on the power and tried to exit the area as fast as possible.

'My bomb exploded just as it reached the roof, and the explosion continued as it penetrated. It took out everything in that warehouse, including the machine guns. I felt very good about the perfect hit, and I'm sure our troops on the ground felt the same way too.'

As naval aviators put the bulk of their efforts in halting anything moving south to reinforce the enemy forces, the communists now realised that they risked being cut off from the north following the Inchon landing. Enemy forces duly commenced a hasty retreat from the Pusan peninsula, using any available routes to flee north. With communist troops now on the move, F4U units relied on fresh intelligence imagery provided by photo-reconnaissance Corsairs and Tigercats to confirm targets for them. With the possibility that pockets of enemy armour and troop transport targets would gravitate towards bridges, tunnels, towns and cities, units put up four flights of four aircraft each so as to maximise the damage inflicted on the NKPA. When the serviceability rate prevented this, another squadron was called in to provide the balance.

For missions against tanks, railway carriages, locomotives or ammunition dumps, the Corsairs would be loaded with two 500-lb GP bombs fitted with instant contact fuses. The tactic often used for such strikes was to position two F4Us at least five minutes ahead of the main force. In addition to the two bombs, these aircraft would also be carrying smoke rockets. On locating the first series of targets, they would fire their rockets. The smoke from the latter would determine the attack direction of the main strike force. This method enhanced the survivability rate amongst Corsair units because the attacking aircraft did not have to loiter over a heavily defended area while selecting their targets.

The two pathfinding Corsairs were seldom bothered by AAA or MiGs, as the NKPA thought that they were decoys. When attacking a dam, the F4U elements of the strike force did not go after the structure, but targeted the associated powerplant. The latter was more susceptible to being seriously damaged by the Corsair's lighter weapon load than the dam itself, which was usually left for the Skyraider units to target with their heavier bombs. In any case, the UN often intended for such powerplant attacks in the early months of the war to merely disrupt electrical supplies, rather than wipe them out.

WEATHER PROBLEMS

Following several months of excellent weather that had allowed Marine Corsair units to fly up to 40 sorties per day between August and late October, November 1950 brought the first cold snap. Conditions worsened as the year drew to a close, the often freezing weather playing havoc with Corsair operations. Lt Col Walter E Gregory, Executive Officer of VMF-212 at Kimpo, provided a vivid picture of operating in low temperatures during the first winter of the Korean War;

'To the best of my knowledge, cold weather operation during a continuing major combat situation was something new for the Marine Corps. World War 2 operations had taken place primarily in the Pacific in tropical weather conditions.

'During the cold winter months, the engine oil in piston-engined propeller types would become so thick that you couldn't pull the prop through. Those F4Us on the flightline that were scheduled to fly would each have their own blow-through heater with flexible tubing to the engine nacelle. The salt water in the western regions of Korea was so cold that slush formed on its surface. Each pilot would therefore have to wear a very thin lightweight immersion suit that was a tiger to maintain. Going north, due to our ordnance load, we flew the sea route whenever possible to avoid flying over friendly areas in that configuration. Accidental release of ordnance on friendly areas was not on our agenda.

'We provided close air support as required. Probably due to peacetime training procedures, the Marine Corps frontline troops were more trusting than other friendly troops, and they would allow us to work directly in front of them. When things got really tight, the others also became a bit more trusting. Of course, we'd be under the control of a specific FAC who'd give us a complete briefing as he observed from overhead. Then a single F4U would make a dry run, with the FAC in continuous contact. If the FAC was satisfied, the flight, following the established flightpath, would come in individually, firing for effect.

'The FAC controlled each of us as we came in, and we observed a simple rule when working in this way – no communication, no drop!

Marine Corps Corsair pilots from VMF-212 show off their new scarves in front of the squadron operations tent at Pohang (K-3) in the early spring of 1951. The unit had only recently come ashore following three months at sea aboard *Bataan* (*National Archives*)

When using napalm, 20 mm cannon or rockets, the runs would be fast and not so steep. With bombs, the angle-of-dive was quite a bit steeper. When the situation on the ground was a bit rough, it was amazing how close we were permitted to come.

'One incident is worth mentioning, as it would pertain to any Corsair pilot working over the frontlines. I was visiting a Marine division at the front, and while standing with the duty FAC in a forward command post, I observed eight F4Us overhead. Everything on the ground was quiet, as it had been thus far in my visit. The FAC informed me that it was my squadron up there. He gave them their instructions and they began their run. Suddenly, this quiet area in front of us erupted with rifle fire, machine gun fire, light cannon fire and maybe more. The number of enemy troops firing on each F4U as it came within range was unbelievable. I yelled at the FAC to tell the pilots to get out of there, but he just shrugged his shoulders and said that this was normal enemy fire! In the cockpit you were unaware you were being fired on, except when you picked up a few small holes in the wings. At a time like this, what the pilot doesn't know sometimes is in his best interest!'

Marine pilots have always been indoctrinated in the close air support of their comrades on the ground. In the pre-World War 2 era, battleships were thought to provide the only close support the Marines needed, but this attitude gradually changed. In the Korean War most Marine ground operations were carried out far out of range of the big guns of the battleships and heavy cruisers. As a result, air support provided the key to softening up enemy strongholds.

The activities of the Marine Corsair pilots are fondly remembered by the troops who depended on this close air support – men like 2Lt Louis Buttell, who was leading the First Platoon, 'Easy Company', 2nd Battalion, 7th Marine Regiment in the Wonju vicinity. He described an event etched in his memory for almost 60 years;

During a lengthy Korean War tour, VMF-214 operated from *Sicily* prior to being based at several South Korean airfields. This photograph was taken on the flightline at Taegu (K-2) in the summer of 1951. Note the F-51s parked in the distance near the control tower (*John Perrin*)

'We were assigned to take a ridge that was heavily fortified with big guns and plenty of enemy troops. We had to cross a valley, and the ground was frozen because of the icy conditions. On the previous day, a flight of F-51 Mustangs had come to help us out, but they weren't effective and we took heavy casualties. They had dropped their ordnance from too high an altitude. Now we were crossing this valley, and we were taking mortar rounds coming from the ridgeline up ahead.

'We immediately made a request for close air support, and we were hoping that some Corsairs would show up. We'd recently learned that, effective 1 January 1951, requests for air support sent to Tokyo were responded to with the first aircraft available. Prior to that time, a Marine forward observer could specify that he wanted a Corsair and that would be the aircraft they'd send.

'To our great relief, a Marine Corsair appeared overhead a short time later and made a run on the bunker that was shelling us. He dropped a canister of napalm that missed the target. We could see the pilot making his turn for a second run, and this time at a much lower altitude. We all swore that he couldn't have been more than a hundred feet off the deck, as we could see his face and goggles. He also slowed down to around 150 knots. This time he didn't miss. He laid that napalm directly on the bunker, setting it on fire and forcing the enemy troops to run out. Most of them were badly burned by the jellied petroleum.

'As the Corsair left the area, we rose and cheered because we knew he'd saved a few lives. We were able to take our objective with light casualties. We never were able to find out the name of that pilot.'

DOGFIGHT!

With close air support missions having the highest priority, the chances of a Marine Corsair encountering any enemy aircraft were remote. All F4U day squadrons spent time operating from land bases in South Korea as well as serving at least one stint aboard the light carriers. Operating from

The pilot checks his straps prior to being catapulted from *Badoeng Strait* during the unit's 1951-52 combat cruise. Assigned to VMF-212 CO Lt Col R L Bryson, this aircraft boasts an impressive mission tally (*Gerald Haddock*)

the ships enabled the pilots to range further up the North Korean coast, and increased the opportunity for aerial combat, even though the NKPAF had virtually ceased to exist after the first few months of combat. By late 1950 F4Us were roaming all the way up to the Yalu River, their pilots itching for a fight.

On 21 April 1951, the 'Checkerboards' of VMF-312 (the unit had gone back to sea aboard CVL-29 in March, taking the place of VMF-212) were steaming up the North Korean coast aboard *Bataan*. The unit's Corsairs were loaded with everything they could carry, including external fuel tanks, 5-in HVARs and two 500-lb general purpose bombs. The pilots were at mission briefing well before first light preparing for a long-range interdiction mission against targets of opportunity. Little did they know that they would encounter four NKPAF Yak-9 fighters whose aggressive pilots were determined to shoot down Marine Corsairs.

Leading the four-ship division was Capt Phillip C DeLong, who had scored 11 kills flying F4U-1s with VMF-212 in the Solomon Islands in early 1944. Before this day was over he would add two more to his tally;

'I led a four-ship flight off the carrier at 0540 hrs. Our mission was armed reconnaissance along the west coast of North Korea. About an hour into the mission, as we got close to Chinnampo harbour, we heard a distress call from one of our pilots who was flying with another VMF-312 division. He radioed that he was baling out, so I immediately notified our carrier's rescue unit to send a helicopter to pick him up. I also sent two of my Corsairs to rendezvous with the chopper while the other division's F4Us remained near the downed pilot. In the meantime, my wingman, Lt Harold Daigh, and I continued on to our original target area.

'We were climbing for altitude, passing through 2000 ft, when we spotted four aircraft approaching us from the northwest at 5000 ft. At this time I had my maps spread out on my lap, and Lt Daigh called them out as F-51 Mustangs. Believing them to be friendly, I didn't pay much attention to them as they turned toward us from the "ten o'clock" position in a loose right echelon formation. They sure looked like Mustangs, but they weren't. I became aware of this when one of their 7.7 mm rounds entered my cockpit, damaging my radio! Taking a few more hits, I realised they were Russian-built Yak-9 piston-engined fighters. While they were concentrating on me, Lt Daigh pulled in behind the last two Yaks.'

Both Corsairs were still loaded with ordnance, as they had not yet engaged any ground targets. Despite this burden, Daigh manoeuvred into position behind the No 3 Yak and opened fire. He did not notice any results, and he turned his attention to the other fighter in the element. A long and accurate burst caught it in the tail, wing root and rear fuselage. As soon as the enemy pilot realised what was happening, he took violent evasive action, but his wing broke off and the stricken fighter plummeted to the ground out of control.

'As soon as I was fired on, I executed a quick split-S to pick up airspeed', Capt DeLong continued. I still had a cockpit full of loose maps, which did nothing for my visibility, and I had to get rid of them fast before I could recover. This was one of the more tense moments of the mission, considering I started the manoeuvre at an altitude of just 2000 ft in a fully-loaded Corsair. But I was able to stow the maps, recover from the dive and make a climbing turn to the left. Although two of the Yaks attacked me again from astern, I was able to turn the tables. While I was in a defensive turn, one of them crossed in front of me from right to left. At that instant, I saw Lt Daigh's first victim crash.'

A second before the Yak passed in front of him, DeLong fired a solid burst and the enemy fighter ran right through his 'wall of fire'. It immediately went into a steep dive, streaming smoke, and hit the ground half-a-mile from where the first Yak had crashed. DeLong jettisoned his bombs but kept the rockets in place, thinking he might need them for the remaining Yaks. As he turned his attention to them, he saw that Daigh was pursuing the third fighter, and the fourth one was on the F4U pilot's tail. DeLong radioed for his wingman to break off and pull hard to the left. As he did so, DeLong opened fire on the trailing Yak. It began smoking from the cockpit area and wing root.

'As I came up on the lead Yak, which Daigh had been trailing, I opened fire and the rounds converged on the forward part of its fuselage. The aircraft started smoking, turned south, did a split-S and then recovered to the west. I followed it throughout this manoeuvre, and continued scoring hits every time I fired. He was trailing thick black smoke, and pieces of the aircraft were falling away. At that point the pilot ceased his evasive tactics, and I knew I had him.'

It was then that DeLong thought it would be a good time to fire his rockets at the stricken fighter. However, when he hit the switch, nothing happened. Moments later the pilot jettisoned his canopy and papers flew out of the cockpit. He then baled out, and his aircraft went straight in. It had taken less than ten minutes to destroy three Yaks and seriously damage a fourth. In fact the wreckage of the latter aircraft was later found in shallow water nearby, so the entire flight of four had been downed to become the Marines' first aerial kills of the war, and the first for the F4U.

STATISTICS

Records show that the Marine Corps flew a total of 34,000 sorties against enemy targets during the first full year of the war. Of this total, 15,000 were flown in support of troops during daylight hours and 3000 at night. The remainder were listed as 'other types', which included armed search and rescue and photo-reconnaissance. During the same period, 48 aircrewmen were killed in action, only three of whom were listed as nightfighter pilots. Although pilots of other Marine Corps types such as the Tigercat, Panther and Skyraider contributed to these statistics, the bulk of the combat sorties were flown by the Corsair squadrons.

The mission tempo did not slacken into the autumn of 1951, with land-based VMF-312 proving to be particularly active in the October-November timeframe. The weather over North Korea during this period ranged from marginal to consistently bad, interspersed with a few days of good flying conditions. With the Chinese attempting to stockpile supplies for an offensive in early 1952, both US Navy and Marine Corps Corsair units were kept busy hammering enemy targets just north of the bomb line. This meant that pilots had to make their attacks from very low level because of the close proximity of friendly troops.

Records for this period show that in October, 26 F4Us were lost, five of which were operated by VMF-312. In November, the losses dropped to 18, two from VMF-312.

VMF-312 pilot Lt Jim Bailey poses beside his loaded F4U-4B at a forward airfield in South Korea. The 5-in HVAR were very effective against Russian-built T-34 tanks (*Jim Bailey*)

'Checkerboard' pilot Capt John J Geuss was in the thick of the action, and on 11 October 1951 he was shot down by ground fire (in F4U-4B BuNo 97486) inland from Cho-do Island whilst on his 25th mission. Geuss recalled;

'We were going after targets just north of the frontlines. We made our high-speed approach over the target, letting down to 10,000 ft and rolling into a dive angle of 40 degrees. I was flying the No 2 position as the division leader's wingman, and our assignment was flak suppression. I fired my rockets in pairs, then released my 500-lb GP bomb at 1500 ft. My airspeed at pullout was 320 knots. Moments later, I felt two slight bumps at approximately 6000 ft, but attributed them to air currents.

'On pulling out, we took a heading of 240 degrees and returned to our rendezvous point. Once we joined up, we headed for the coast, and ten minutes later I noticed my oil pressure was at 65 psi – I immediately notified my division leader. We were about ten miles east of Cho-do Island. Within a couple of minutes my pressure had dropped to 50 psi, and I told my leader that I was going to try a wheels-up landing on the island. There was some cloud cover over the area, so lead went down to check it out. He radioed back that the northwest corner of the island was clear, with a nice beach to land on. By this time, my oil pressure was down to 35 psi. I made one pass over the beach and heard one of the guys in my division radioing for the SA-16 "Dumbo".

'As I let down through 1000 ft and began to lower my flaps, I noticed that oil was flowing under the flap near the left wing root. I glanced at my gauges again and saw that the pressure was now down to 25 psi. Continuing my approach, I cleared a hill on the northern end of the island and landed on the beach. My fighter skidded for at least 600 ft as if it was on a greased surface, and just before it came to a halt, the Corsair veered to the right and stopped in about 18 inches of water. By this time a crowd of civilians had gathered, and several approached me. The rest of my division circled overhead, ready to make a strafing attack if it appeared that I was about to be taken prisoner.

'There must have been several hundred people in the crowd that gathered, but at no time did it occur to me that they might be hostile. It had been my personal observation while covering downed pilots that if the Koreans were unfriendly they'd stay out of sight and fire from cover, especially with several armed Corsairs overhead.

'Twenty-five minutes after I landed on the beach at Cho-do, I was picked up by the "Dumbo" amphibian. As it taxied in close to the shore, it got stuck in the sand where the water was only a couple of feet deep. However, it didn't have any trouble getting free, and I was immediately taken back to Seoul City airfield (K-16).'

The statistics that Capt Geuss compiled during his tour in Korea were typical for the average Corsair pilot during this period. His personal log book states that he flew 78 combat missions over North Korea, and his expenditure of ordnance was as follows – 54 napalm canisters totalling 8100 gallons, 257 5-in HVARs, 215 100-lb GP bombs, 21 250-lb bombs, 16 500-lb bombs and 49 1000-lbs bombs. He also received the DFC for a mission flown on 22 November 1951 that involved a four-aircraft division diving below low cloud to assist friendly troops suffering heavy casualties. Geuss recalled what happened next;

'The controller was able to mark the target with a smoke rocket, but we couldn't gain much altitude due to the low ceiling. We never exceeded 220 knots at any point in the mission, and it was very uncomfortable flying at such slow speeds over enemy territory. We effectively became a slow-moving target for small arms fire. We made four runs, dropping two napalm canisters and six 100-lb bombs apiece. The ordnance was dropped right on target, and we all but wiped out the enemy force posing the threat. We received thanks from several sources for our effectiveness on that mission.'

MiG ENCOUNTER

By mid-1952, with the threat of communist invasion having been stymied by many months of convoy interdiction sorties, Marine Corsair operations had switched to concentrating on supporting UN and RoK troops that were holding the frontline. For pilots who later tried to recall particular missions from this period, details pertaining to the number of sorties flown and the type of ordnance delivered seems to have been lost over the passage of time. But one thing is for sure. They faced withering ground fire on each and every mission, and as the distance north from the bomb line increased so too did the calibre of the AAA!

During September 1952, there was one mission that stood out from the norm because it involved enemy resistance from the air, rather than from the ground. By this stage of the war, the only communist aircraft

Between 21 April and 21 July 1952, VMF-312 flew combat missions from *Bataan*. These 'Checkerboard' Corsairs are seen parked on the aft flightdeck of the light carrier during a rare liberty port call in Japan (*Robert Howard*)

encountered south of the Yalu River were MiG-15s, and they had the potential to outnumber UN aircraft on any given day.

Between August 1950 and December 1952, the light carrier *Sicily* supported strikes into North Korea by F4U units VMF-214 (1950), VMF-323 (1951) and VMA-312, which operated from the ship between 4 September and 19 October 1952.

On 10 September 1952, an interdiction and close air support mission called for maximum effort, and the ship launched a large number of the 'Checkerboards'' F4U-4Bs. Capt Jesse G Folmar was leading one division, and during the course of the mission he and his wingman, Lt Walter E Daniels, would be involved in an historic encounter with some aggressive MiG-15s. Taking off at 1610 hrs, they were ordered to attack a troop concentration on the south side of the Taedong River, close to Chinnampo. Capt Folmar recalled how events unfolded;

'As we crossed the coast and headed into enemy territory, we began executing a tactical weave at 10,000 ft. Arriving over the target area, we observed no activity, so we continued to fly reconnaissance in the area of the Taejon estuary. As we started to bank over a small island off the coast, I caught a glimpse of two MiG-15s in the early stages of setting up for a firing pass on us. They were in loose section formation, so I steepened the angle of my banking turn into them, while at the same time increasing power. I jettisoned all external ordnance and fuel tanks and then switched to the guard channel to report that we were being attacked by MiGs. I told Lt Daniels to fly a much tighter weave, and not to let the communist jets out of his sight.

'Seconds later, I spotted two more of them closing rapidly from my "eight o'clock". I turned hard to the left, trying to bring my guns to bear before they could open fire, but due to their rapid closure, I was unable to do so. Their tracers were overshooting us, so I reversed my bank to the

Many Corsairs ended up like this when they returned to their carriers with heavy battle damage. This F4U-4B was assigned to VMA-312 aboard *Sicily*, and it was one of four Corsairs lost by the unit during October 1952 (*Marshall Armstrong*)

right and turned inside one of the MiGs as he started a climbing left turn. I pulled up and got him squarely in my gunsights, giving him about 20 mils' lead. I then triggered off a long five-second burst with my four 20 mm cannon. I could tell that I had him boresighted by the blinking flashes along the left side of his fuselage. A grey trail of fuel vapour began to stream from the MiG, and this quickly turned into billowing black smoke. He nosed over slightly and seemed to lose acceleration. Seconds later the pilot ejected, and he tumbled

Rear Admiral E G A Clifford visits *Badoeng Strait* on 10 December 1952 to present awards to pilots from VMA-312 for their outstanding work against North Korean targets during October and November of that year (*Marshall Armstrong*)

through the air in what appeared to be a ball of smoke. When his parachute opened, I could see his "G" suit burning from head to foot. I glanced down and saw the flaming MiG hit the water vertically.'

Both Folmar and Daniels resumed their defensive weave, and soon four more MiGs joined the fight, strung out in a loose column of two sections. Suddenly, the odds facing the Corsair pair were stacked even greater against them. Folmar decided to break off for home, and he ordered a hard break to the left and down;

'I had just started picking up good diving speed when I saw balls of tracer passing on my left. At that instant I felt a severe jolt and explosion in my left wing. My aircraft began to shudder as if in a high-speed stall. I glanced over and saw that my left aileron and about four feet of my left wing were gone. Also, the top of the left wing was gutted to the inboard side of my inboard 20 mm gun. My damaged aeroplane was trying to roll to the left, although the control column was placed in a full right position. This led to my decision that it would too hazardous to attempt a landing back on *Sicily*, so I decided to bale out.'

Folmar transmitted the search and rescue distress signal and repeated his position, before getting ready to bale out. Whilst he was doing this another MiG made a firing pass at him, but its shells went wide. At 3000

A division of AU-1s from VMA-323 forms up over the frontlines in Korea during a close sir support mission in late 1952. Aircraft assigned to the 'Death Rattlers' always displayed the 'WS' tail code. The unit operated a mixed force of 12 AU-1s and 12 F4U-4Bs from Pyongtaek (K-6) during the final year of the war (*Jack Dunn*)

The 'Devilcats' of VMA-212 also flew AU-1s in combat from mid 1952. This version of the Corsair was designed specifically for the ground attack mission, and just 111 examples were built in 1952-53. The aircraft's R-2700-83W engine generated 2300 hp, and it was armed with four 20 mm cannon, thus making the AU-1 a devastating weapon for strafing attacks. This aircraft was photographed at Kimpo (K-14) during the spring of 1953 (*Doug Carter*)

Marine Corps pilot Lt Russ Janson, pictured here at Pyongtaek, flew AU-1s with VMF-212 in 1952-53 (*Russ Janson*)

ft he rolled out of the right side of the cockpit and fell clear. Just as he pulled the D-ring on his parachute, he heard an ear-splitting noise, and he looked up to see another MiG firing at his stricken Corsair. Seven MiG-15s remained in the area, but they departed as soon as Folmar hit the water. He estimated that he was in the sea for about eight minutes before being rescued by an SA-16 Albatross 'Dumbo'.

Records show that Jesse Folmar's F4U-4B (BuNo 62927) was one of nine Marine Corps Corsairs to be lost in action in September 1952 – six of these were AU-1s from the 'Devilcats' of VMA-212 (all VMF-designated Corsair units had switched to VMA in late 1952). The US Navy lost four, one of which was an F4U-5N nightfighter assigned to VC-3 Det E aboard *Princeton*. This took the month's total of Corsair losses to 13, which was just below the average of 15 for the 37 months of the war. Losses in October were even lower, with 11 F4Us being destroyed, including six from the Marines Corps.

Three of the four day Marine Corps F4U squadrons and the nightfighter unit that arrived during the war's early stages were still active in July 1953. The exception was VMA-312, which was relieved on 8 June 1953 when its carrier USS *Bairoko* (CVE-115) docked at Itami. Its replacement was VMA-332 'Polka Dots', embarked in USS *Point Cruz* (CVE-119). The latter unit was issued with VMA-312's F4U-4Bs in Japan prior to going into combat aboard CVE-119.

The following month the 'Death Rattlers' of VMA-323 were also withdrawn, enjoying a brief stay at Itami AB before moving to MCAS Atsugi and eventual transportation back to CONUS. By then it had achieved the distinction of being the longest-serving Marine tactical (VMA/VMF) air squadron of the Korean War. VMA-323's final sorties on 2 July 1953 took its overall tally in Korea to 20,827 and 48,677.2 combat hours since the unit arrived in-theatre in August 1950.

Although the Marine Corps committed just six Corsair units to the conflict in Korea, the exploits of these squadrons in the first ten months of the war are the stuff of legend. Their dedication to protecting troops on the ground once the conflict became stalemated in the spring of 1951 also made the MAG F4U units the most popular when close air support was urgently called for. Finally, the loss of 260 Marine Corps Corsairs in Korea between August 1950 and July 1952 is testament to the ferocity of the action that these units saw throughout the conflict.

VMA-332 'Polka Dots' replaced VMA-312 'Checkerboards' in Korea just weeks before war's end. Issued with the latter unit's F4U-4/Bs, it flew combat missions exclusively from USS *Point Cruz* (CVE-119) whilst in-theatre (*Art Beasley*)

Marine Corps pilot Capt Jerry Coleman flew a combined total of 120 combat missions during World War 2 and the Korean War. Serving with VMA-323 in the latter conflict, Coleman was also an all-star second baseman with the New York Yankees who was eventually inducted into the Hall of Fame. He is seen here in the cockpit of his F4U at Pyongtaek in 1953 (*Peter Mersky*)

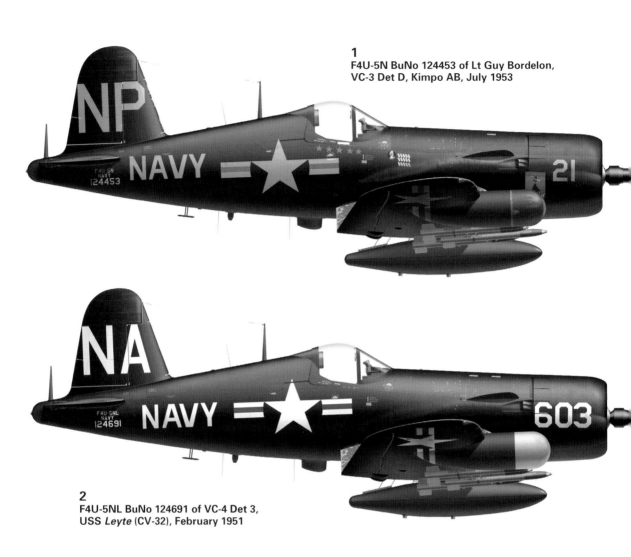

1
F4U-5N BuNo 124453 of Lt Guy Bordelon,
VC-3 Det D, Kimpo AB, July 1953

2
F4U-5NL BuNo 124691 of VC-4 Det 3,
USS *Leyte* (CV-32), February 1951

3
F4U-5P BuNo 122019 of VC-61 Det,
USS *Philippine Sea* (CV-47), May 1951

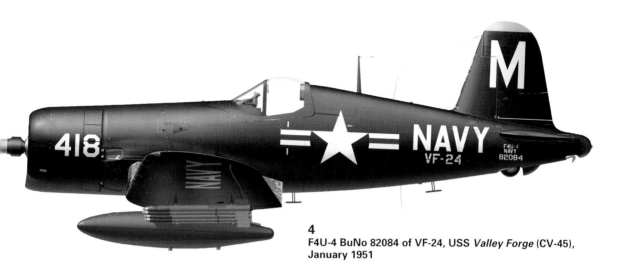

4
F4U-4 BuNo 82084 of VF-24, USS *Valley Forge* (CV-45),
January 1951

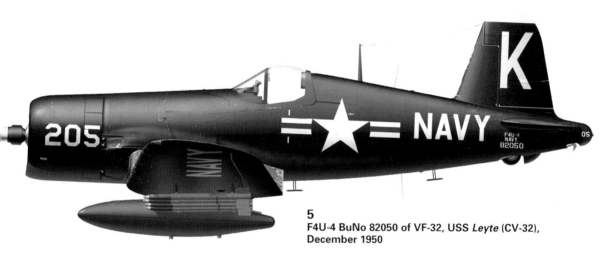

5
F4U-4 BuNo 82050 of VF-32, USS *Leyte* (CV-32),
December 1950

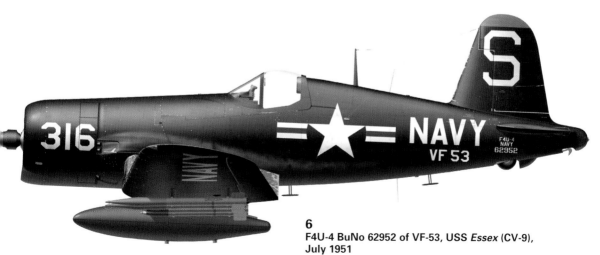

6
F4U-4 BuNo 62952 of VF-53, USS *Essex* (CV-9),
July 1951

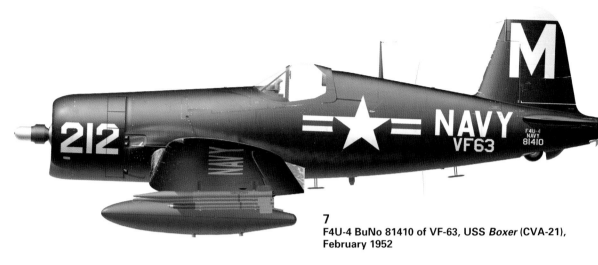

7
F4U-4 BuNo 81410 of VF-63, USS *Boxer* (CVA-21),
February 1952

8
F4U-4 BuNo 82080 of VF-64, USS *Valley Forge*
(CV-45), February 1951

9
F4U-4 BuNo 81975 of VF-74, USS *Bon Homme
Richard* (CVA-31), November 1952

10
F4U-4 BuNo 81251 of VF-113, USS *Philippine Sea*
(CV-47), February 1952

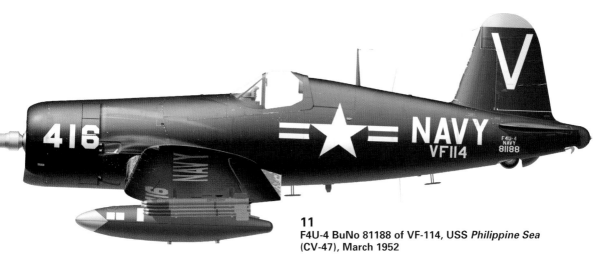

11
F4U-4 BuNo 81188 of VF-114, USS *Philippine Sea*
(CV-47), March 1952

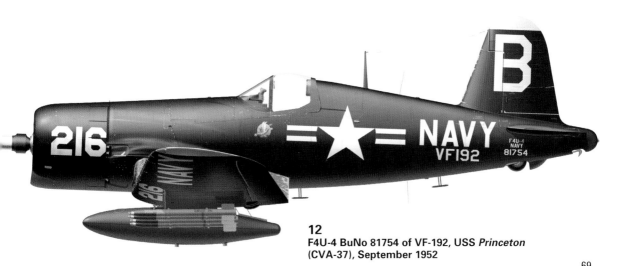

12
F4U-4 BuNo 81754 of VF-192, USS *Princeton*
(CVA-37), September 1952

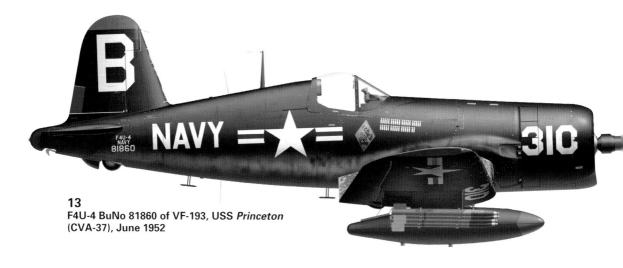

13
F4U-4 BuNo 81860 of VF-193, USS *Princeton*
(CVA-37), June 1952

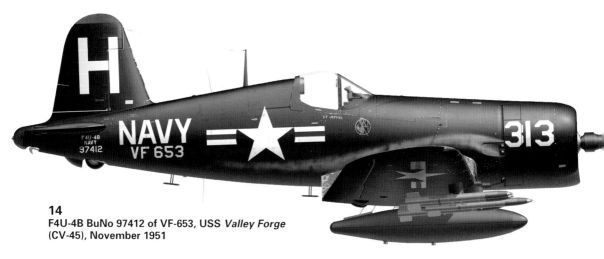

14
F4U-4B BuNo 97412 of VF-653, USS *Valley Forge*
(CV-45), November 1951

15
F4U-4B BuNo 81568 of VF-713, USS *Antietam*
(CV-36), January 1952

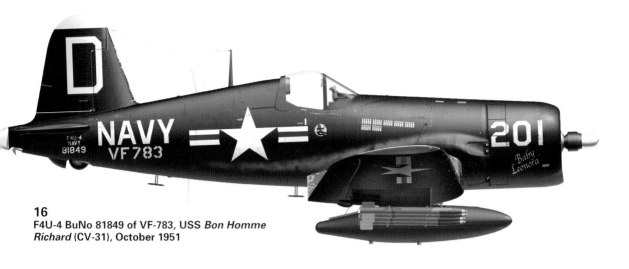

16
F4U-4 BuNo 81849 of VF-783, USS *Bon Homme Richard* (CV-31), October 1951

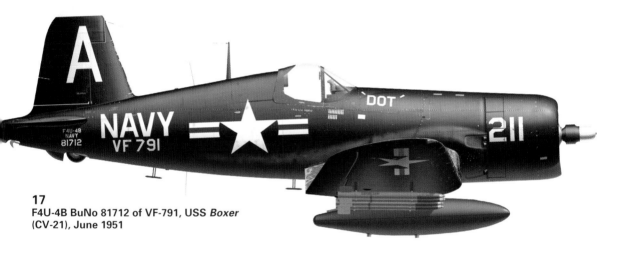

17
F4U-4B BuNo 81712 of VF-791, USS *Boxer* (CV-21), June 1951

18
F4U-4 BuNo 81673 of VF-821, USS *Princeton* (CV-37), August 1951

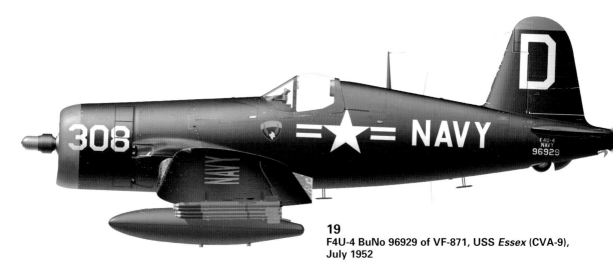

19
F4U-4 BuNo 96929 of VF-871, USS *Essex* (CVA-9),
July 1952

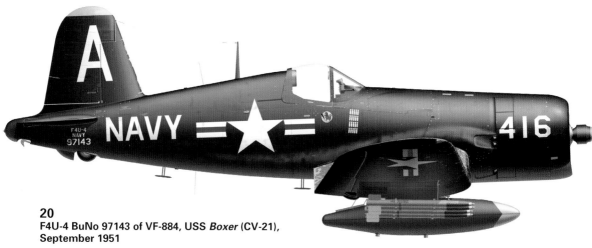

20
F4U-4 BuNo 97143 of VF-884, USS *Boxer* (CV-21),
September 1951

21
F4U-4B BuNo 82176 of VMF-212, USS *Rendova*
(CVE-114), September 1951

22
AU-1 BuNo 129359 of VMA-212, Pyongtaek (K-6),
May 1953

23
F4U-4B BuNo 97479 of VMF-214, USS *Sicily*
(CVE-118), September 1950

24
F4U-4B BuNo 62940 of VMF-214, Yonpo (K-27),
December 1950

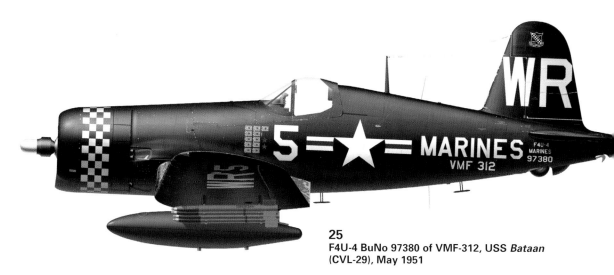

25
F4U-4 BuNo 97380 of VMF-312, USS *Bataan*
(CVL-29), May 1951

26
F4U-4B BuNo 62927 of VMA-312, Pyongtaek (K-6),
September 1952

27
F4U-4 BuNo 96845 of VMF-323, USS *Sicily*
(CVE-118), June 1951

28
AU-1 BuNo 129350 of VMA-323, Pyongtaek (K-6),
February 1953

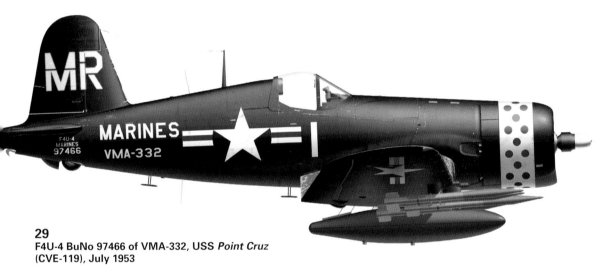

29
F4U-4 BuNo 97466 of VMA-332, USS *Point Cruz*
(CVE-119), July 1953

30
F4U-5N BuNo 123176 of VMF(N)-513, Kangnung
(K-18), October 1951

31
F4U-5N BuNo 123180 of VMF(N)-513, Kangnung
(K-18), June 1951

32
F4U-5P BuNo 122168 of VMJ-1, Pohang (K-3),
August 1952

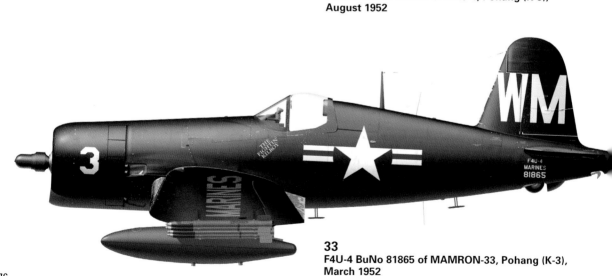

33
F4U-4 BuNo 81865 of MAMRON-33, Pohang (K-3),
March 1952

NIGHTFIGHTER OPERATIONS

The F4U-5N nightfighter had an early impact on the war. VMF(N)-513 arrived in the Far East in early August 1950 via an aircraft carrier, and one day out from reaching port, the squadron launched its aircraft for Itazuke AB, Japan, because there was no room for them on the overcrowded South Korean airfields. Itazuke was the nearest Japanese base to the Korean Peninsula, and from there they would range out and hit targets north of the Pusan perimeter. Some of these early missions took them deep into North Korea.

The unit's CO at the time, Maj J Hunter Reinburg, recalled what he and his squadron were facing in August and early September 1950;

'Our F4U-5Ns were equipped with better radar than that used by US nightfighter units during the latter stages of World War 2. Besides being able to detect other aircraft, it had two other outstanding features – it could "map" the terrain up to 80 miles ahead and it could detect a ground-based beacon, thereby providing azimuth and distance for almost 100 miles. We also had four 20 mm cannon mounted in the wing, compared to the older models with their six 0.50-cal machine guns. When the 20 mm guns were fired during my first mission over Korea, the recoil was like several mules kicking and the radar went blank! Needless to say, the factory people got to work on some better shock mountings.

'In our first few weeks of night strikes over the Pusan perimeter's Naktong front, we discovered that our mere presence over enemy lines did a great deal of good, even when we were not actively engaging a target. We got so proficient at uncovering their movements that the enemy thought we had a super electronic way of detecting his every move! The NKPA kept its lights out, and stopped all activity when we were about.'

In 1950-51, the North Koreans tried several different tactics to thwart the night intruders attacking their trucks and trains. The mountainous

During the early stages of the war, the F4U-5Ns of VMF(N)-513 'Flying Nightmares' were based at the Pusan (K-1) and Pohang (K-3) airfields. Later, they operated from Kunsan AB (K-8), on the west coast (*Hans Petermann*)

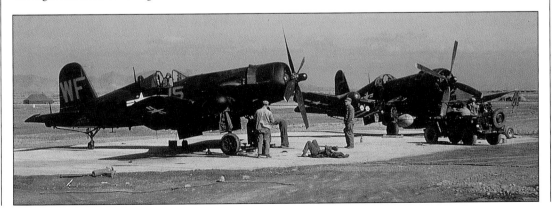

One of VMF(N)-513's nightfighter Corsairs heads north late in the afternoon to catch truck movements at dusk. Such missions saw these aircraft ranging all over North Korea in search of trains and trucks on the move. During the early stages of the war, the unit's 'WF' tail codes and individual aircraft numbers were applied in white, but these were switched to low-visibility red in 1951 (*Lynn Williams*)

Capt Lynn Williams poses beside his fully-loaded F4U-5N prior to flying a night harassment mission over North Korea. His aircraft is armed with 5-in HVARs, and it also boasts a centreline fuel tank for increased endurance when hunting for targets on enemy roads. This photograph was taken at Itazuke AB, Japan, in late 1950 (*Lynn Williams*)

terrain meant that all the main roads and railway lines were located in the valleys. To be effective, therefore, F4U-5Ns and F7F-3Ns had to fly at lower altitudes, leading the enemy to string cables from ridge to ridge. One F-82 and several F-51s were lost as a result, and other aircraft came back with cables dangling behind them that had been caught on the leading edges of the wing. However, none of these moves could deter the F4U-5N pilots.

The 'Flying Nightmares' of VMF(N)-513 were strictly land-based, and they did not operate from carriers during the war. Once space became available in South Korea, they moved up from Japan, which allowed them much more loiter time over enemy territory.

The most lucrative targets were usually found in the deepest valleys on a moonless night when movement was at its peak. In such cases, most nightfighters worked under flares to illuminate the targets. The down side of this was that away from the flares it was pitch black, making it almost impossible for a pilot to tell when the valley was coming to an end. Most Corsair nightfighter pilots worked closely, and effectively, with the USAF 'Firefly' squadron flying C-47 flare ships from Kimpo AB.

Lt Harold E Roland was a Marine F4U-5N pilot who encountered heavy AAA on several occasions when attacking targets in certain areas;

'AAA fire, while heavy in certain areas, was a factor we could work around. If, under the first flare, we recognised a village or road configuration that was a known AAA hot spot, we would simply move up the road. Fortunately, the enemy gunners always used telltale tracers, and usually they would be shooting as we entered the flare light. As the streams of tracers came pouring up, it was safer to duck down low and go further down the road for a mile or so, calling the flare ship to follow you.

'We could recognise the type of guns by the nature of the tracers. The orange balls that floated up in pairs were the heavier guns firing explosive shells from twin mounts. The reddish streams were smaller calibre weapons, and you could tell how close they were getting by the speed of the shells. If the tracers floated up, you had nothing to fear. If they were streaks of fire snapping by the cockpit, they had your range. In the later months, the gunners – probably Chinese – would wait while you worked under the flares for a time, and they had your pattern calibrated. Then they would cut loose with everything. You would suddenly find yourself dazzled by streams of tracers from below and the flares floating down from above. In

that demonic glow, the vertigo problem became intense. On half of my missions, I was hit by small-calibre stuff – my aircraft was struck by an explosive round just the once.

'Our bomb loads were very effective in cutting railway lines and stopping the lead vehicles of convoys. We specifically targeted the roads well north of the bomb line in the Sibyon-ni and Chorwon areas. They were typically thick with Chinese trucks, as they were constantly trying to build up enough supplies for their troops to stage an offensive. They would run with their headlights on in convoys of ten to fifteen, with short separations between convoys. From a distance, their headlights would glow in the sky not unlike a busy road system in the US. They were all fair game, but the small, abrupt mountains in the area, and of course never knowing exactly where even the flat ground was, caused us to be cautious about going right down without flare support.

'I learned in my first few flights that pickling off bombs and rockets or strafing from 1000 ft produced poor results. The truck drivers were bold, learning from the other night intruders that ordnance delivered from that altitude was not really a serious threat. They would usually keep driving when you tried to attack from a "safe" altitude. Even if they stopped and turned their lights off, we could not claim anything. Our standard was that you must see a truck burning in order to claim it. Sometimes we would strafe up and down a convoy and they would be immersed in total darkness, with no indication of what effects our guns had. Thus was born the joke that "they were carrying a load of wet cabbages".

'We F4U-5N pilots discussed the situation, and agreed that we had to hit an individual truck to do the damage needed. We then abandoned the tactic of bombing or strafing up and down a road that contained trucks and instead singled out individual vehicles, or tightly bunched groups. The F7F Tigercat pilots were at a disadvantage here due to their larger, less manoeuvrable aircraft.

'Fortunately, we had C-47 flare ships assigned to our sectors along the main supply routes. These aircraft were carrying hundreds of 1,000,000-

MAG-33 was the first Marine air group to deploy to Korea, and one of its three Corsair squadrons was nightfighter-equipped VMF(N)-513. While its sister-squadrons flew their first missions from carriers, the 'Flying Nightmares' operated from land bases in South Korea and Japan. This photograph was taken on the ramp at Pusan AB in December 1950 (*Marvin Wallace*)

candlepower magnesium flares. If their aircraft happened to get hit by ground fire, it would have become an instant, giant flare lighting the countryside like a small sun. Without these heroes, we could not have done our job, as their continuous dropping of flares at lower altitudes allowed us to stay down and work over the trucks. A lot of our outstanding successes in this mission had to be credited to them.'

The Marine Corps had an advantage in night operations because it could field two different and very effective ground attack nightfighters in the F4U-5N and

Pilots of VMF(N)-513 pose for the camera at Pusan AB in April 1951. The Chinese had already entered the war and the frontlines had finally stabilised around the 38th Parallel by the time this photograph was taken (*Ray Stewart*)

F7F-3N – the latter had entered the war in September 1950 with VMF(N)-542. On 20 February 1951, this changed when members of VMF(N)-542 were sent back to CONUS to commence their conversion training onto the new F3D Skyknight jet nightfighter. VMF(N)-513 was duly ordered to bring all the Tigercats under its control, which meant that one squadron would be operating full complements of two different aircraft types. This merger was carried out without any operational interruption, and the pressure on Chinese logistics routes never slackened.

In all, the Chinese planners had to contend with US Navy F4U-5Ns from VC-3 (embarked in detachment strength on all large-deck carriers), the Marine Corps' F4U-5Ns and F7F-3Ns and a large number of USAF B-26 Invaders. All operated in specific sectors so that there was no mission overlap, thus greatly reducing the chances of a mid-air collision. The effectiveness of their night offensive forced the enemy to deploy a great many large-calibre AAA weapons to protect their assets.

Night attack pilots usually came down into the valleys, maintaining a high air speed, which meant that the gunners were always tracking slightly behind them. A few aircraft disappeared without trace, indicating that they were shot down by ground fire or had been flown into the side of a mountain on a dark night.

One of the more experienced VMF(N)-513 F4U-5N pilots, Capt William J Webster, recalled one of his best nights over North Korea;

'This mission was flown on the night of 15-16 March 1951 when I was working with a flare ship up in the Sibyon-ni area. We flushed out a large truck convoy moving south. Flying low under the flares, I was able to take out 25 trucks, and the only reason my score wasn't higher was because I ran out of ammunition. I was relieved by the squadron

VC-3 was the US Navy's primary nightfighter squadron, with detachments serving aboard most fleet carriers stationed off the North Korean coast throughout the war. One of its F4U-5N Corsairs is pictured here preparing to launch at last light for a night intruder mission against enemy truck convoys (*Tailhook Association*)

CO, Lt Col James R Anderson, who confirmed my kills. Considering that my Corsair only carried 800 rounds, and the guns could fire at the rate of 700 rounds per minute, I was very effective with short bursts on each pass. This equated to about 32 rounds per truck, which is pretty accurate.

'A short time later, I was out in the same area. There was a full moon and the trucks were running without their lights. This called for us to fly what I felt was the most dangerous type of mission – hugging the road right above treetop level following surface reflections in the moonlight. When we passed over a black spot on the road, which usually meant a vehicle, we pulled up and did a quick wingover for a strafing pass.

'Due to the reduced visibility, we were well within firing range when we got the pipper on the black image for a quick burst of 20 mm. I was passing this road junction when I noticed several black spots close together, and as I pulled up for my wingover, there was a long burst of heavy calibre automatic fire from the road junction below. When I came back for my strafing pass, two separate vehicles opened up at me. At the time, I felt I had the advantage in that as long as they were shooting at me with tracers, I knew exactly where to put my pipper. They were only shooting at the sound of my engine. Each time I pulled up in a right wingover, they would adjust their fire to the left, and so on.

'That night I was carrying six 265-lb fragmentation bombs under my wings, and after a couple of firing passes, I switched to bombs and dropped two strings of three on each pass. There were immediate secondary explosions and no more automatic weapons fire, so I moved on up the road looking for more targets.'

A DANGEROUS ASSIGNMENT

As previously mentioned in this chapter, both the US Navy and Marine Corps fielded single specialised squadrons equipped with the F4U-5N that were capable of operating at night, and they contributed significantly to the closure of many roads and railway lines during the conflict. The US Navy's VC-3 employed detachments aboard most of the aircraft carriers serving in the war, and they had the additional responsibility of defending these vessels against night attack. The Marines usually operated their F4U-5Ns from South Korean land bases at Pusan West (K-1) and Kunsan (K-8). They operated in specific sectors to ensure that every mile of enemy territory was covered by at least one type of aircraft.

While flying at night might have been considered to be safer than facing daytime AAA and, possibly, MiG-15s, in reality this was not the case. The mountainous terrain of North Korea and the bitterly cold winter weather made night flying the most dangerous assignment that any pilot could be given. All roads and railway lines passed through valleys, and even with the light of a full moon it was difficult to distinguish where the valleys ended and the mountains began. Flying on a moonless night meant that the danger doubled. Nevertheless, the night interdiction pilots from all branches of the military did an exceptional job, and the convoys and trains they disabled were pounced upon at first light by the day fighter-bombers.

The enemy did everything it possibly could to ensure the safe passage of supply trucks. They came up with a system reminiscent of the days of the 'Flying Tigers' in China in World War 2, when air raid warnings were

Ens Russell Novak of VC-3 Det F checks his F4U-5N on the deck of *Kearsarge* during the vessel's 1952-53 combat cruise. He achieved great success attacking truck convoys at night over North Korea while flying with the det (*Russ Novak*)

A VC-3 Det D F4U-5N moves into position for launching on a rare daylight close air support mission from *Princeton* in 1953. Note how its white tail codes and star and bar have been blackened to reduce their visibility at night (*Wayne Russell*)

made by individuals on the ground without radios. The North Koreans and Chinese devised a similar system using spotlights operated from the tops of ridges. Ens Russell Novak of VC-3 Det F flew F4U-5Ns from *Kearsarge* as part of CVG-101 in 1952-53. Here, he recalls a tactic employed to counter this warning system;

'The enemy was moving most of its supplies and equipment at night, even though night attack aeroplanes were making it costly for them to do so. They just kept coming regardless of losses. Up in the hilly terrain, the roads invariably wound around the mountains and through the adjacent valleys. It was standard operating procedure to station a watch person on the tops of these ridge lines with a hand held spotlight that put out a beam that could be seen on the roads below. This person would, upon hearing an aeroplane engine, turn off the spotlight to warn the convoy below. They, in turn, would immediately turn off all headlights to avoid being seen by the aircraft. I was well aware of this tactic, and decided to try something to counter it.

'On one of my missions, when I saw a spotlight in the distance, I went to full power and pulled the nose up to gain as much altitude as I could. I was at such a distance that I saw the light before the operator heard my engine, but he did hear me when I climbed. Fortunately, I knew exactly where he was. After the sound of my engine disappeared, he turned the light back on to signal the trucks to start moving again. I then dropped the nose and pulled back on the throttle to cut down on any noise and then extended my landing gear to lose speed as my dive steepened.

'As I plummeted down into the valley, I increased the power as I was already on top of them. A second later, I released my bombs at a dangerously low altitude, taking out several trucks in the convoy. With the airspeed I had gained in the dive, I got the heck out of there as quick as I could. The next day, my plane captain called me up to take a look at my Corsair. There were tree branches poking out of the landing gear wheel wells! I was young and foolish at that time, and it was one of the closest calls I had on the cruise.'

The mountainous nature of the North Korean terrain made tactical air warfare very difficult even during the day. The night missions were far

A pristine F4U-5N from VC-3 Det D is seen here 'chocked and chained' on *Princeton's* flightdeck during a liberty port call in early 1953 (*Wayne Russell*)

A pair of enlisted crewmen from VC-3 Det E pose in front of a Corsair nightfighter aboard *Princeton* whilst the carrier was alongside at NAS North Island prior to the vessel's departure on its 1952 Korean War cruise (*Evan Baney*)

more hazardous. When the F4U-5Ns did penetrate the dark valleys, their pilots had to face heavy AAA, especially in places where damaged railway lines would be difficult to repair, as well as overhead busy road junctions. VMF(N)-513's second CO in Korea, Lt Col James R Anderson, offered a comment on the hazards faced by his pilots;

'The accuracy of the ground fire we faced can never be understated. It was rumoured that for every UN aircraft a Chinese gunner shot down, he was given ten days liberty in Shanghai, and judging from the volume and accuracy of the AAA fire, the entire Chinese army was trying to get those ten days off. The defensive firepower increased as time went on in the war. As our effectiveness increased against their efforts to move supplies, so did the number of automatic weapons.

'When working under the flares, the communists had more of a target to shoot at, but when the moon dimly lit the valleys, they were shooting at our sound. This usually meant that the rounds passed harmlessly behind us. Fortunately for the UN ground forces, the Chinese had a very difficult time in re-supplying their troops because they had to move over treacherous roads in mountainous terrain. But they never let that hinder their efforts, remaining stubbornly persistent until war's end.'

US NAVY DETs

US Navy carrier-based nightfighter detachments typically deployed with four F4U-5Ns and up to six pilots per air group. For such small dets any losses were acutely felt, and replacement pilots and aircraft had to be quickly brought in. Lt Don Shelton was a VC-3 pilot in 1950-51, and he recalled replacing losses to *Princeton's* detachment;

'One of our units had lost two aircraft, and my buddy, Lt Harley Mayfield, and I were ordered to fill in the gap. We got priority transportation to the Far East and were taken out to the carrier by the COD, which was a World War 2-vintage TBM Avenger. Its pilot had had no instrument training and we were in the winter season, so the flight kept us wide-awake as we flew in and out of snow clouds.

'Once over *Princeton*, we were told to divert to Taegu AB because of ice and snow covering the flightdeck. Once we made it there, we had to circle because a Marine F9F was being cleared for take-off. We later found out that the Panther pilot was baseball legend Ted Williams. We eventually made it over to *Princeton*, and Lt Mayfield and I commenced our combat careers flying in the most appalling of weather conditions. The air temperature on the flightdeck was always near zero and the wind chill factor was worse than that.

'It was in such conditions that we had a rather chilling, and very unusual, experience on an early March 1951 mission. We made the scheduled 0300 hrs launch for an interdiction mission that covered road routes from Wonsan north to Hungnam.

'Approaching Wonsan at 8000 ft, we circled and then headed north. A few minutes later Lt Mayfield announced that his engine had quit and, seconds later, that he was getting ready to bale out. I told him that the island in the middle of the harbour was friendly. He then said that he had climbed halfway out of the cockpit when his engine had started running again, so he was going to try and make it back to the carrier. He made the turn and I kept on heading north.

'It didn't take long to find some action, and I disposed of a five-truck convoy before heading back in the direction of Wonsan. At that point my engine also quit, and I too was at 8000 ft! I immediately radioed the ship that I was considering baling out, but I managed to get the engine re-started on the primer at about 1000 rpm. One of VC-11's AD-4W "Guppies" working in the area heard my transmission and offered to accompany me back to *Princeton*. Once I was over the ship, I talked with our LSO and elected to try what essentially amounted to a dead stick landing. I was at 3000 ft at the "180", all the while on the primer ticking over at 1000 rpm. It was enough to get me safely down on the deck. Our maintenance people looked into my problem, and it turned out to be fuel/water frappe (foam) in the new model belly strainer.'

Such blockages could have been the reason for the loss of several F4Us at this time, most of which resulted in the death of the pilots involved. Shelton could easily have been lost had he been forced to bale out over open water;

'On that mission, I wasn't wearing my "poopy suit" because of the limited time we'd had before take-off, and the fact that they were so hard to get into. After that close call, I was a religious wearer of the "suit", which was mandatory because it kept you from freezing to death in the bitter cold water, at least until a rescue helicopter could reach you.

'For anyone not familiar with the cockpit of a F4U-5N Corsair, the two buttons for the engine starter and primer were side by side and mounted on the lower right panel so that you had to push forward on the buttons rather than push down. You have no idea how sore your fingers could get under prolonged pushing forward on those two buttons.

'I've been asked several times if I had ever had a chance of a night kill. One night I had an "unknown" on my radar, and while I was closing I thought I'd better test my guns just in case, but they wouldn't fire. It was a problem with the 20 mm guns that was soon remedied.'

Although the NKPAF had virtually ceased to exist as a viable fighting force within weeks of the conflict commencing, it was still able to conduct a lengthy campaign of night-time nuisance raids against USAF bases. The aircraft it used were piston-engined types ranging from the La-9/11 fighter through the Yak-18 primary trainer to the antiquated Po-2 biplane. Lives were lost and damage was done in these raids, which presented the USAF with a dilemma. Geared to counter high-performance aircraft such as the MiG-15, the fighter units in-theatre were particularly baffled as to how to engage 80-knot biplanes that were quickly dubbed 'Bed-Check Charlies'. Flying low along moon-lit valleys to foil UN radar, the Po-2s were quickly getting the upper hand.

While a Marine Corps F3D-2 did shoot down a Po-2 (and six MiG-15s) and an F-94 flew through one, causing the destruction of both aircraft, the Yak-18s and the biplanes were generally too slow for the Skyknights and Starfires to effectively intercept. The Fifth Air Force duly sought the loan of US Navy F4U-5Ns, and on 17 June 1953, VC-3 Det D of *Princeton's* CVG-15 was assigned to Kimpo AB (K-14) near Seoul. Commanded by 31-year-old Lt Guy P Bordelon, the det was later transferred to the Marine Corps airfield at Pyongtaek (K-6), 30 miles south of the capital, which was better equipped to service the Corsairs.

Bordelon had joined the US Navy in 1942 and had seen service with TBM Avenger-equipped VC-87 embarked in USS *Corregidor* (CVE-58) in the Pacific theatre in 1944-45. Posted to VC-3 in 1952, he embarked with his det aboard *Princeton* in late January 1953. During the course of the eight-month cruise, Bordelon got the chance to justify his nickname of 'Lucky Pierre', and write himself into the history books as the US Navy's only ace of the Korean War.

With his det having been ashore for 12 days, Bordelon took off on yet another night sortie on 29 June in his F4U-5N (BuNo 124453), which he called *ANNIE-MO* after his wife. He was accompanied by Lt(jg) Ralph Hopson. A short while later, a ground radar detected a hostile aircraft over Asan-Man, near Seoul. Although radar-equipped, the nightfighter pilots were under orders to make a visual identification before opening fire. A moon-lit night such as this one made the task easier, and having closed to within visual range, Bordelon identified the intruder as a Yak-18. Ordered to attack, he quickly destroyed the aircraft with a 56-round burst from his 20 mm cannon.

The only Corsair pilot to become an ace during the Korean War was Lt Guy Bordelon, who led F4U-5N-equipped VC-3 Det D assigned to *Princeton*. His kills were scored against night heckling Yak-18s and La-9/11s in June-July 1952 whilst his det was shore-based at Kimpo and Pyongtaek (*Guy Bordelon*)

Soon afterwards, Bordelon, now alone because Hopson had experienced problems with his radar, was vectored onto a second target, which he identified as yet another Yak-18. Bordelon closed in from behind and fired a long burst which set fire to the Yak. The aircraft shed a wing and exploded when it hit the ground.

On the night of 1/2 July, Bordelon (again in BuNo 124453) intercepted two La-9/11 fighters and succeeded in destroying them both. Finally, on the night of 16/17 July, Bordelon shot down another La-11

to become the only non-jet US ace of the Korean War. He was awarded the Navy Cross for his efforts.

Half a century later, Bordelon's unique feat was to be remembered in another way. On behalf of the American Fighter Aces' Association, artist Roy Grinnell vividly recorded the Corsair pilot's achievement on 16/17 July 1952 in a painting entitled *Night Kill*. Putting his signature to the artwork, 'Lucky Pierre' recalled the night's events;

'I gave a "tally-ho" and reported that the contact was definitely an unfriendly aircraft. Joint Operations Center gave me clearance to fire just as the enemy aircraft began to bank hard to port. As we passed Kaesong, he suddenly rolled level, and I gave him a long burst of 20 mm HEI (high explosive incendiary) cannon fire. I saw a wing coming off and pulled left as he blew up with a tremendous explosion. Then, turning right and circling, I could see the bright splash of fire on the ground as the La-11 impacted.'

The US Navy operated F4U-5Ns until the end of the war, although the nightfighter version of the F2H Banshee had entered limited service in Korea by then. Nevertheless, VC-3 with its Corsairs remained the only active all-weather and nightfighter squadron to see extensive combat operations. The Marine Corps, however, phased out its F4U-5Ns soon after the F3Ds arrived in 1952, and by war's end operated day fighter models only. The damage inflicted on the enemy by this specialised version of the Corsair may never be known, but it must have been significant. The day fighter-bomber pilots could certainly vouch for this, as they routinely attacked trains and truck convoys that had been blocked by nightfighters during the early hours.

Lt Guy Bordelon (standing behind the officer with his hands in his pockets) is interviewed at Kimpo after his ace-making exploits, achieved in this F4U-5N, BuNo 124453. The fighter was left behind at Kimpo when Det D was sent back to CVA-37, and it was written off in an accident at the base on 30 August 1953 whilst being flown by a USAF Reserve pilot (*John Ferebee*)

VC-3 was a unique US Navy fighter unit operating during the post-World War 2 era. Based at Moffett Field, California, it was comprised of over 100 highly-trained nightfighter pilots. Detachments were embarked on all the fleet carriers operating during the Korean War. This F4U-5N of VC-4 Det E is seen aboard *CVA-37* in 1952 (*Wayne Russell*)

APPENDICES

APPENDIX A

US NAVY F4U CORSAIR DEPLOYMENTS

USS *Valley Forge* (CV-45)
First cruise – 1 May 1950 to 1 December 1950
CVG-5

VF-53	F4U-4B	tail code S
VF-54	F4U-4B	tail code S
VC-3 Det C	F4U-5N	tail code NP
HedRon-1 Det	F4U-5P	tail code AZ

USS *Philippine Sea* (CV-47)
First cruise – 24 July 1950 to 7 April 1951
CVG-11

VF-113	F4U-4B	tail code V
VF-114	F4U-4B	tail code V
VC-3 Det 3	F4U-5N	tail code NP
VC-61 Det	F4U-4P	tail code PP

USS *Boxer* (CV-21)
First cruise – 24 August 1950 to 11 November 1950
CVG-2

VF-23	F4U-4	tail code M
VF-24	F4U-4/B	tail code M
VF-63	F4U-4	tail code M
VF-64	F4U-4	tail code M
VC-3 Det-3	F4U-5N	tail code NP
VC-61 Det	F4U-4P	tail code PP

USS *Leyte* (CV-32)
First cruise – 6 September 1950 to 3 February 1951
CVG-3

VF-32	F4U-4	tail code K
VF-33	F4U-4	tail code K
VC-4 Det 3	F4U-5N/NL	tail code NA
VC-62 Det 3	F4U-5P	tail code PL

USS *Princeton* (CV-37)
First cruise – 9 November 1950 to 29 May 1951
CVG-19

VF-192	F4U-4	tail code B
VF-193	F4U-4	tail code B
VC-3 Det F	F4U-5N	tail code NP

USS *Valley Forge* (CV-45)
Second cruise – 6 December 1950 to 7 April 1951
CVG-2, which cross-decked with CVG-11 from USS *Philippine Sea* (CV-47) on 28 March 1951 and CV-45 returned to San Diego, California, on 7 April with CVG-11 embarked

VF-24	F4U-4	tail code M
VF-63	F4U-4	tail code M
VF-64	F4U-4	tail code M
VF-65	F4U-4	tail code M
VC-3 Det	F4U-5N	tail code NP
VC-61 Det F	F4U-4P	tail code PP

USS *Boxer* (CV-21)
Second cruise – 2 March 1951 to 24 October 1951
CVG-101

VF-791	F4U-4	tail code A
VF-884	F4U-4	tail code A
VC-3 Det F	F4U-5NL	tail code NP

USS *Philippine Sea* (CV-47)
Second cruise – 28 March 1951 to 9 June 1951
CVG-2

VF-24	F4U-4	tail code M
VF-63	F4U-4	tail code M
VF-64	F4U-4	tail code M
VC-3 Det	F4U-5N	tail code NP
VC-61 Det	F4U-5P	tail code PP

USS *Bon Homme Richard* (CV-31)
First cruise – 10 May 1951 to 17 December 1951
CVG-102

VF-783	F4U-4	tail code D
VF-874	F4U-4	tail code D
VC-3 Det G	F4U-5N	tail code NP

USS *Princeton* (CV-37)
Second cruise – 31 May 1951 to 29 August 1951
CVG-19X

VF-821	F4U-4	tail code B
VF-871	F4U-4	tail code B
VC-3 Det	F4U-5N	tail code NP

USS *Essex* (CV-9)
First cruise – 26 June 1951 to 25 March 1952
CVG-5

VF-53	F4U-4/B	tail code S
VC-3 Det B	F4U-5NL	tail code NP

USS *Antietam* (CV-36)
First cruise – 8 September 1951 to 2 May 1952
CVG-15

VF-713	F4U-4	tail code H
VC-3 Det D	F4U-5N	tail code NP

USS *Valley Forge* (CV-45)
Third cruise – 15 October 1951 to 3 July 1952
ATG-1

VF-653	F4U-4/B	tail code H
VC-3 Det H	F4U-5N/NL	tail code NP

USS *Philippine Sea* (CV-47)
Third cruise – 31 December 1951 to 8 August 1952
CVG-11

VF-113	F4U-4	tail code V
VF-114	F4U-4	tail code V
VC-3 Det C	F4U-5N/NL	tail code NP

USS *Boxer* (CVA-21)
Third cruise – 8 February 1952 to 26 September 1952
CVG-2

VF-63	F4U-4	tail code M

VF-64	F4U-4	tail code M
VC-3 Det A	F4U-5N	tail code NP

USS *Princeton* (CVA-37)
Third cruise – 21 March 1952 to 3 November 1952
CVG-19

VF-192	F4U-4	tail code B
VF-193	F4U-4	tail code B
VC-3 Det E	F4U-5N	tail code NP

USS *Bon Homme Richard* (CVA-31)
Second cruise – 20 May 1952 to 8 January 1953
CVG-7

VF-74	F4U-4	tail code L
VC-4 Det 41	F4U-5N	tail code NP

USS *Essex* (CVA-9)
Second cruise – 16 June 1952 to 6 February 1953
ATG-2

VF-871	F4U-4	tail code D
VC-3 Det I	F4U-5N	tail code NP

USS *Kearsarge* (CVA-33)
Cruise – 11 August 1952 to 17 March 1953
CVG-101 (re-designated CVG-14 4 February 1953)

VF-884	F4U-4	tail code A
VC-3 Det F	F4U-5N	tail code NP

USS *Oriskany* (CVA-34)
Cruise – 15 September 1952 to 18 May 1953
CVG-102

VF-874	F4U-4	tail code D
VC-3 Det G	F4U-5N	tail code NP

USS *Valley Forge* (CVA-45)
Fourth and final cruise – 20 November 1952 to 25 June 1953
CVG-5

VF-92	F4U-4	tail code N
VC-3 Det B	F4U-5N	tail code NP

USS *Philippine Sea* (CVA-47)
Fourth and final cruise – 15 December 1952 to 14 August 1953
CVG-9

VF-94	F4U-4	tail code N
VC-3 Det M	F4U-5N	tail code NP

USS *Princeton* (CVA-37)
Fourth and final cruise – 24 January 1953 to 21 September 1953
CVG-15

VF-152	F4U-4	tail code H
VC-3 Det D	F4U-5N	tail code NP

USS *Boxer* (CVA-21)
Fourth and final cruise – 30 March 1953 to 28 November 1953
ATG-1

VF-44 (from CVA-39 on 30/6/53)	F4U-4	tail code F
VC-3 Det H	F4U-5N	tail code NP

USS *Lake Champlain* (CVA-39)
Cruise – 26 April 1953 to 4 December 1953
CVG-15

VF-44 (to CVA-21 6/53 and back to CVA-39 10/53) F4U-4		tail code F

APPENDIX B

US MARINE CORPS F4U CARRIER DEPLOYMENTS

USS *Sicily* (CVE-118)
On station – 4 July 1950 to 5 February 1951

VMF-214 (1 August 1950 to 13 November 1950)	F4U-4B	tail code WE

USS *Badoeng Strait* (CVE-116)
On station – 14 July 1950 to 7 February 1951

VMF-323	F4U-4/B	tail code WS

USS *Bataan* (CVL-29)
On station – 16 November 1950 to 25 June 1951

VMF-212 (11 December 1950 to 5 March 1951)	F4U-4B	tail code LD
VMF-312 (5 March 1951 to 6 June 1951)	F4U-4	tail code WR

USS *Sicily* (CVE-118)
On station – 12 May 1951 to 12 October 1951

VMF-323 (5 June 1951 to 20 September 1951)	F4U-4/B	tail code WS

USS *Rendova* (CVE-114)
On station – 8 July 1951 to 22 December 1951

VMF-212 (22 September 1951 to 6 December 1951)	F4U-4/B	tail code LD

USS *Badoeng Strait* (CVE-116)
On station – 15 September 1951 to 1 March 1952

VMF-212	F4U-4/B	tail code LD

USS *Bataan* (CVL-29)
On station – 27 January 1952 to 26 August 1952

VMA-312 (21 April 1952 to 21 July 1952)	F4U-4/B	tail code WR

USS *Sicily* (CVE-118)
On station: 8 May 1952 to 4 December 1952

VMA-312 (4 September 1952 to 19 October 1952)	F4U-4B	tail code WR

USS *Badoeng Strait* (CVE-116)
On station – 19 July 1952 to 27 February 1953

VMA-312 (19 October 1952 to 9 February 1953)	F4U-4/B	tail code WR

USS *Bataan* (CVL-29)
On station – 28 October 1952 to 26 May 1953

VMA-312 (9 February 1953 to 8 May 1953)	F4U-4	tail code WR

USS *Bairoko* (CVE-115)
On station – 12 January 1953 to 24 August 1953

VMA-312 (9 May 1953 to 8 June 1953)	F4U-4/B	tail code WR

USS *Point Cruz* (CVE-119)
On station – 11 April 1953 to 18 December 1953

VMA-332	F4U-4/B	tail code MR

APPENDIX C

SUMMARY OF KOREAN WAR CORSAIR LOSSES IN INCREMENTS OF 50

US Navy

No 1 – 3 July 1950, VF-53 F4U-4B BuNo 96809
Engine failure on launch from USS *Valley Forge* (CV-45). Pilot rescued by helicopter uninjured, but KIA 25 September 1950

No 50 – 18 February 1951, CVG-2 (unit unknown) F4U-4 (BuNo unknown)
Ditched at sea in minefield following engine failure during mission from USS *Valley Forge* (CV-45). Pilot Ens T R Tvede rescued uninjured by boat from USS *Ozbourn* (DD-846)

No 100 – 30 July 1951, VF-821 F4U-4 BuNo 81877
Engine stalled on approach to USS *Princeton* (CVA-37) and aircraft exploded on impact with water. Pilot KIA

No 150 – 18 January 1952, VC-3 Det D F4U-5NL BuNo 124551
Struck aft 5-in gun mount while approaching deck of USS *Antietam* (CV-36), resulting in total loss, but pilot uninjured

No 200 – 13 June 1952, VC-3 Det H F4U-5N (BuNo unknown)
Crashed soon after take-off from USS *Valley Forge* (CV-45). Pilot rescued uninjured

No 250 – 29 June 1953, VF-94 F4U-4 BuNo 92928
Hit by AAA during mission from USS *Philippine Sea* (CVA-47). Pilot Lt J R Caufield ditched in sea and rescued by helicopter

No 258 (final US Navy Corsair loss) – 26 July 1953, VF-152 F4U-4 BuNo 81834
Hit by AAA during reconnaissance mission from USS *Princeton* (CVA-37). Pilot Lt William C Blackford KIA

US Marine Corps

No 1 – 8 August 1950, VMF-323 F4U-4B BuNo 97483
Struck by another aircraft that jumped landing barrier aboard USS *Badoeng Strait* (CVE-116). Pilot injured

No 50 – 2 January 1951, VMF-214 F4U-4B BuNo 97393
Engine failure on take-off from USS *Sicily* (CVE-118). Pilot rescued by USS *John A Bole* (DD-755)

No 100 – 2 May 1951, VMF-323 F4U-4B BuNo 63044
Hit by AAA, pilot baled out and captured, but repatriated during Operation *Big Switch*

No 150 – 31 July 1951, VMF-212 F4U-4B BuNo 63014
Lost power on take-off and ditched. Pilot Lt Allan T Wood rescued by fishing boat

No 200 – 5 December 1951, VMF-312 F4U-4B BuNo 97407
Destroyed when hit while parked by crippled AD-4L landing at Kangnung (K-18)

No 250 – 9 June 1952, VMF-323 F4U-4B BuNo 62934
Exploded during mission and seen to crash and burn. Pilot 1Lt John J McBride III listed KIA

No 300 – 8 February 1953, VMA-323 AU-1 BuNo 129392
Hit by small arms fire over target and suffered engine failure. Crashed and burned north of Yonch-On. Pilot Capt Joseph Januszewski listed KIA, and remains later recovered

No 315 (final Marine Corps Corsair loss) – 24 July 1953, VMA-332 F4U-4 BuNo 81008
Ditched on take-off from USS *Bairoko* (CVE-115). Pilot 1Lt Arthur Beasley rescued by helicopter

COLOUR PLATES

1

F4U-5N BuNo 124453 of Lt Guy Bordelon, VC-3 Det D, Kimpo AB, July 1953

This aircraft, christened *ANNIE-MO*, was credited with the destruction of five NKPAF night intruder aircraft in June-July 1953 whilst operating from Kimpo AB. It was flown by the US Navy's sole Korean War ace, Lt Guy Bordelon, who was also CO of VC-3 Det D, embarked in USS *Princeton* (CVA-37) but sent ashore to protect airfields around Seoul from slow-flying night intruders. Built in February 1950, BuNo 124453 served with VC-4 prior to being issued to VC-3 in August 1952. The fighter was left behind at Kimpo when Det D was sent back to CVA-37, and it was written off in an accident at the base on 30 August 1953 whilst being flown by a USAF Reserve pilot.

2

F4U-5NL BuNo 124691 of VC-4 Det 3, USS *Leyte* (CV-32), February 1951

VC-4 sent just two dets of F4U-5NLs to Korea during the conflict. The first of these was Det 3 embarked in *Leyte* between September 1950 and February 1951, which included this late-build aircraft within its ranks. Serving exclusively with VC-4 throughout its five years in service, BuNo 124691 also made cruises aboard USS *Tarawa* (CVA-40) and USS *Valley Forge* (CVA-45) in 1953, *Leyte* and *Tarawa* once again in 1954 and finally CVA-32 in 1955. It was stricken in June 1956.

3

F4U-5P BuNo 122019 of VC-61 Det, USS *Philippine Sea* (CV-47), May 1951

Photo-reconnaissance missions for US Navy carrier task groups were handled by small detachments of F4U-4/5Ps from VC-61 and HedRon 1 during the first year of the war, although the Corsairs were replaced by F9F-2P and F2H-2Ps from mid 1961 onwards. The recce-Corsair's finest hour came when US Navy and Marine Corps aircraft conducted extensive photo surveys of Inchon harbour in advance of the hugely successful amphibious assault in mid September 1950. Built in July 1948, this F4U-5P served with VC-62 prior to being transferred to VC-61 in mid 1950. Participating in CV-47's second war cruise, and assigned to CVG-2, this aircraft remained in Japan when the carrier returned to CONUS in June 1951. Issued to MAG-33's HedRon, it saw further action in Korea until shipped back to California in February 1952. Transferred to VCJ-1, the aircraft returned to US Navy control in June 1953 when it was assigned to VF-13. The Corsair was stricken in November 1955.

4

F4U-4 BuNo 82084 of VF-24, USS *Valley Forge* (CV-45), January 1951

VF-24 was in the thick of the action during the first 18 months of the war, flying combat missions from three aircraft carriers (*Boxer* in 1950, *Valley Forge* in 1950-51 and *Philippine Sea*, also in 1951) in that time whilst assigned to CVG-2. BuNo 82084 is seen in typical unit markings worn by VF-24 throughout this period. Built in June 1945, it served with VMF-322 during 1946-48, before spending two years in storage. Assigned to VF-24 as an attrition replacement in December 1950, the Corsair saw combat with the unit until transferred to VF-791 aboard CV-21 in May 1951 when CVG-2 headed home. Reassigned to VF-653 and embarked in CV-45 in January 1952, BuNo 82084 was hit by AAA and its pilot forced to ditch in Wonsan harbour on 10 June 1952.

5

F4U-4 BuNo 82050 of VF-32, USS *Leyte* (CV-32), December 1950

Although VF-32 'Gypsies' participated in just one war cruise in Korea, the unit undertook some of the most dangerous sorties of the entire conflict in defence of Marines fighting near the Chosin Reservoir in late 1950. One of these missions, on 4 December, resulted in VF-32's Lt(jg) Thomas Hudner being awarded the Medal of Honor when he attempted to rescue squadronmate Ens Jesse Brown, who was trapped in the cockpit of his Corsair after it had been shot down near Hagaru-ri. Hudner crash-landed BuNo 82050 alongside the downed F4U-4 (BuNo 97231), but failed in his bid to free Brown from the wreckage of the Corsair. Built in June 1945, BuNo 82050 had served with VBF-19 (1945), VMF/VMF(N)-114 (1946-47) and VMF-451, prior to being placed in storage until September 1950, when it was issued to VF-32.

6

F4U-4 BuNo 62952 of VF-53, USS *Essex* (CV-9), July 1951

VF-53 undertook two F4U cruises during the war, seeing combat from the decks of *Valley Forge* in 1950 and *Essex* in 1951-52. One of the first US Navy F4U units thrown into action over North Korea, VF-53 used the letter 'S' as its tail code, with blue trim on the tail tip and propeller hub, on both cruises. Built in January 1957, this aircraft served with VMF-224 (1947-48), VMF-452 (1948), VMF-312 (1949-50) and VMT-2 (1950), prior to being issued to VF-53 in March 1951. It was written off in a flying accident on 27 July 1951.

7

F4U-4 BuNo 81410 of VF-63, USS *Boxer* (CVA-21), February 1952

The 'Fighting Redcocks' of VF-63 flew combat missions from three different carriers – *Boxer* twice (1950 and 1952), *Valley Forge* (1950-51) and *Philippine Sea* (1951). Built in April 1945, this Corsair served with VBF-95 (1945), VBF-153 (1945), VBF-81 (1945), VMF-122 (1946) and VMF-212 (1946-

48), before spending two years in storage. Issued to VF-63 in September 1951, the aircraft completed the unit's final war cruise aboard CVA-21, and was then transferred to VMA-251 in December 1952. BuNo 81410 was stricken in August 1953.

8
F4U-4 BuNo 82080 of VF-64, USS *Valley Forge* (CV-45), February 1951
VF-63 and VF-64 served as sister-squadrons within CVG-2 during their four Korean War cruises. Assigned to 'Freelancers' pilot Lt Jack Kendall, this aircraft saw plenty of action during CVG-2's deployment, which started aboard CV-45 in December 1950 and ended with the air group embarked in CV-47 in June 1951. Built in June 1945, BuNo 82080 served with VMF-211 (1945-46) prior to being placed in storage until July 1950, when it was assigned to VF-193. Transferred to VF-64 four months later, the aircraft remained in Japan when CV-47 returned to CONUS. It was passed on to VMF-212 in Korea in September 1951 and subsequently issued to VMF-312 in February 1952. The aircraft flew missions with this unit from the light carriers *Bairoko* and *Bataan* off the North Korean coast from February to May 1952. Returned to CONUS in August of that year, the Corsair served with the Naval Air Reserve Training (NART) unit at Los Alamitos, California, from 1953 to 1955, before being stricken in April 1956.

9
F4U-4 BuNo 81975 of VF-74, USS *Bon Homme Richard* (CVA-31), November 1952
East Coast-based VF-74 'Be-Devilers' completed just one combat cruise to Korea with CVG-7, embarked in *Bon Homme Richard*, between May 1952 and January 1953. The squadron was the only complete Corsair unit within the air group, which also boasted a handful of F4U-5Ns assigned to VC-4 Det 41. Delivered in June 1945, BuNo 81975 served with VMF-211 (1945-46) and the Naval Air Reserve unit in New York (1947-48), before being placed in storage until September 1950. The fighter was then issued to Reserve-manned VF-783, where it remained until June 1951. Following more time in storage, the F4U was allocated to VF-74 in April 1952, and it remained with this unit until June 1954. Retired the following month, the Corsair was stricken in April 1956.

10
F4U-4 BuNo 81251 of VF-113, USS *Philippine Sea* (CV-47), February 1952
One of the first US Navy Corsair units to see action over North Korea in August 1950, the 'Stingers' of VF-113 completed two combat cruises. Flying its F4U-4Bs from *Philippine Sea*, the squadron hit targets in North Korea from 5 August through to late March 1951. The unit's second war deployment, again with CVG-11, was made aboard 'Phil Sea' in 1952, this time with F4U-4s. Unit aircraft were always identified by the letter 'V' on the vertical stabiliser and blue trim on the

propeller hub, fin tip and drop tank. Boasting a mission tally and unit badge beneath the cockpit, this aircraft was assigned to VF-113 from October 1951 through to May 1952. Built in March 1945, BuNo 81251 served with VBF-86 (1945), VMF-222 (1947), VMF-122 (1947) and VF-173 (1950). It experienced combat with VF-64 and VF-23 aboard CV-21 during the vessel's first war cruise in the latter half of 1950, before transferring to VF-923 in December of that year. Assigned to VF-113 in October 1951, it was passed on to VMA-312 in August 1952, and survived more combat with this unit from the light carrier *Sicily* through to October of that year. Returning to CONUS the following month, BuNo 81251 was written off in a flying accident on 14 September 1953 whilst assigned to Marine Aircraft Engineering Squadron 12.

11
F4U-4 BuNo 81188 of VF-114, USS *Philippine Sea* (CV-47), March 1952
Like VF-113, VF-114 also flew F4U-4Bs on its first cruise with CV-47 in 1950, and the unit had re-equipped with 'Dash Fours' by the time its second deployment commenced aboard the same carrier on New Year's Eve 1951. Both cruises came at critical times in the war, with the first seeing VF-114 heavily involved in the defence of the Pusan perimeter, and the highlight of the second being the decisive strikes against the hydroelectric dams on the Yalu River. BuNo 81188 was built in March 1945 and delivered to VBF-95. It then served with VBF-153 (1945), VBF-81 (1945), VF-6B (1947), VF-4B (1948) and VF-23 (1950), prior to joining VF-114 in August 1951. The aircraft was transferred to VF-193 as an attrition replacement in August 1952, and it completed its second combat cruise with the unit aboard *Princeton*. Passed on to VF-92 four months later, the Corsair was involved in its third war cruise in just 12 months when it embarked with the unit in CVA-45 in November 1952. BuNo 81188 returned to CONUS ahead of VF-92 in March 1953, and it was stricken five months later.

12
F4U-4 BuNo 81754 of VF-192, USS *Princeton* (CVA-37), September 1952
VF-192 logged two combat cruises aboard *Princeton*, the first from November 1950 through to May 1951, followed by a March to November 1952 deployment. Both were with CVG-19. Equipped with F4U-4s throughout the war, VF-192 used the 'B' tail code with white trim on the vertical stabiliser and propeller hub – also note the unit's winged dragon emblem beneath the cockpit of this machine. Built in May 1945, BuNo 81754 served with VF-10 (1945), VF-14 (1945), VF-17 (1946) and VF-5B (1946), prior to joining MAG-11 (1947). Assigned to VMT-2 in 1947-48, the Corsair was stored through to January 1951, when it was issued to VF-821. Eight months later it joined VF-64, before being transferred to VF-192 in March 1952 and embarking on CVG-19's final war cruise later that same month. The fighter was hit by AAA

and crashed into a hill near Kuwon'go-ri on 12 September 1952.

13
F4U-4 BuNo 81860 of VF-193, USS *Princeton* (CVA-37), June 1952

VF-193 was VF-192's sister-squadron, and it participated in both cruises undertaken by CVG-19 aboard *Princeton*. Unit aircraft also featured the air group's 'B' tail code, as well as VF-193's blue trim in all the usual locations. This well-weathered F4U was also adorned with a bomb tally and unit emblem below the cockpit. Built in June 1945, the fighter served with VBF-150 (1945) and VBF-17 (1946), prior to being stored until May 1950. It was then issued to VMF-211, who passed it on to VMT-2 eight months later. In May 1951, BuNo 81860 was transferred to VF-713, and in August of that same year it joined VF-193. The aircraft deployed with the unit aboard CVA-37 in March 1952, and it was downed by AAA near Wonsan harbour on 15 June – the pilot baled out and was rescued.

14
F4U-4B BuNo 97412 of VF-653, USS *Valley Forge* (CV-45), November 1951

VF-653 was one of a handful of F4U-equipped Reserve squadrons mobilised following the outbreak of war in Korea. Originally from Akron, Ohio, the unit embarked in CV-45 as ATG-1's sole F4U squadron in October 1951. VF-653 was led into combat by Lt Cdr Cook Cleland, who had won two Cleveland National Air Races flying a Corsair in the late 1940s. The unit had six pilots killed or posted MIA during seven months of combat in what proved to be its only war cruise. Built in May 1946, this aircraft served with VFB-75 (1946) and VF-4B (1946-47), after which it was in storage until May 1950. Issued to VMF-311, the Corsair joined VMF-312 two months later, followed by VMT-2 in August and VMF-235 the following month. Returning to VMT-2 in November, the aircraft was assigned to VF-653 in September 1951 and saw combat with the unit until sent to Japan for overhaul three months later. transferred to VMF-323 in January 1952, BuNo 97412 suffered structural failure after being hit by its own bomb blast during a close air support mission near Sinwon on 26 March 1952. Its pilot, 2Lt Joseph H Kuney Jr, died in the subsequent crash.

15
F4U-4B BuNo 81568 of VF-713, USS *Antietam* (CV-36), January 1952

Antietam undertook one combat cruise to Korea between 8 September 1951 and 2 May 1952, embarking CVG-15 for the first of its two war deployments. All of the air group's fighter and attack units were Reserve-manned, with VF-713 (mobilised in Denver, Colorado, on 1 February 1951) being the sole F4U-equipped unit in CVG-15 – VC-3 Det D was also embarked with its F4U-5Ns. Built in May 1945, this aircraft served with VF-75B (1945), VBF-75 (1945-46), VMF-122 (1946),

VMF/VMF(N)-114 (1947) and VMF-461 (1948), prior to being placed in storage. Assigned to VF-23 in January 1950, BuNo 81568 saw combat with this unit whilst embarked in *Boxer* between September and November. Transferred to VF-713 in August 1951, the aircraft returned to CONUS with the unit in May 1952 and was stricken exactly a year later.

16
F4U-4 BuNo 81849 of VF-783, USS *Bon Homme Richard* (CV-31), October 1951

VF-783, from Los Alamitos, was yet another Naval Air Reserve squadron called to active duty, being mobilised on 2 August 1950. One of four Reserve-manned fighter and attack units assigned to CVG-102 and embarked in *Bon Homme Richard*, VF-783 undertook a seven-month cruise to Korea between 10 May and 17 December. The unit subsequently re-equipped with F9F-5s in early 1952 and completed a second combat cruise aboard *Oriskany* in 1952-53. This aircraft was unusual in that it featured a nickname on its cowling, as well as an impressive bomb tally and unit emblem beneath the cockpit. BuNo 81849 was built in May 1945 and served with VMF-115 (1945-47), prior to being stored until March 1951. It was then issued to VF-783 and completed the unit's sole combat cruise with the Corsair. Transferred to VF-41 in June 1952, BuNo 81849 was subsequently assigned to VMF-333 in November 1953 and retired in March of the following year. It was stricken in April 1956.

17
F4U-4B BuNo 81712 of VF-791, USS *Boxer* (CV-21), June 1951

Hailing from Memphis, Tennessee, VF-791 undertook its solitary combat cruise with CVG-101 aboard *Boxer* between 2 March and 24 October 1951. An aggressive squadron, it logged 1250 sorties and 3600 combat hours during the deployment. Credited with the destruction of 175 bridges, 140 trucks, 125 railway wagons and several hundred buildings, VF-791 was nicknamed the 'Rebels' due to its Confederate Flag-inspired emblem. Most of the targets listed here were destroyed by the unit during CVG-101's participation in Operation *Strangle*, which saw a large number of bridges dropped and countless railway lines severed in North Korea in 1951. Another Reserve aircraft to boast a name, BuNo 81712 was built in May 1945 and flown by VBF-10 (1945), VBF-14 (1945), VBF-17 (1946) and VF-6B (1946-47). Assigned to several training units between 1947 and 1950, it was issued to VF-791 in November of that year, and remained with the unit through to February 1952. Transferred to VMA-332 in October 1952, the Corsair was eventually retired in May 1954 and stricken in April 1956.

18
F4U-4 BuNo 81673 of VF-821, USS *Princeton* (CV-37), August 1951

VF-821 was one of the first Reserve squadrons to

be mobilised at its New Orleans base in July 1950. It completed one brief cruise (31 May to 29 August 1951) aboard CV-37 as part of CVG-19X, when units assigned to the latter air group were issued with the aircraft flown by CVG-19, which had been embarked in *Princeton* since November 1950 – the two air groups undertook a back-to-back turnaround in Japan between 29-31 May 1951. By this time, the frontlines had almost stabilised, which meant that Corsair units were hitting targets deeper into North Korea. VF-821 would transition to F9F-2s in early 1952 and return to Korea aboard *Essex* later that year. BuNo 81673 was accepted by the US Navy in June 1945 and flown by VBF-20 (1945), VBF-17 (1946) and VF-6B (1946-47), after which it spent three years with training units. Transferred to VF-192 in August 1950, the aircraft saw extensive combat with CVG-19 from *Princeton* between November 1950 and May 1951, when the unit's total complement of F4U-4s was transferred to VF-821. The fighter remained with the squadron until it was passed on to VF-33 in August 1952, after which it joined NART St Louis, Missouri, in May 1953. Retired in March of the following year, the Corsair was stricken in February 1956.

19

F4U-4 BuNo 96929 of VF-871, USS *Essex* (CVA-9), July 1952

Based in Oakland, California, VF-871 was another Reserve squadron mobilised in early 1951. It made two combat cruises with the F4U, the first being aboard *Princeton* from 31 May through to 29 August 1951 as part of CVG-19X – the unit lost five aircraft and three pilots during this brief three-month deployment. VF-871 was the only F4U-4 unit in ATG-2 when the unit made its second cruise embarked in *Essex* between 16 June 1952 and 6 February 1953. Built in July 1945, BuNo 96929 was flown by VMF-217 (1946) and VMF-214 (1946-47) prior to being placed in storage. Issued to VF-193 in August 1950, the Corsair saw combat with this unit until passed on to VF-871 in May 1951 as part of the back-to-back turnaround between CVG-19 and CVG-19X. Returning to CONUS with the Reserve squadron, the aircraft completed only two months of VF-871's second war cruise prior to being shipped back home. Transferred to VF-42 in August 1952, BuNo 96929 joined NART Niagara Falls, New York, in November 1953, and was eventually retired a year later. The fighter was stricken in April 1956.

20

F4U-4 BuNo 97143 of VF-884, USS *Boxer* (CV-21), September 1951

VF-884 'Bitter Birds' from Olathe, Kansas, made two Korean War tours. The first, from 2 March to 24 October 1951, took place with CVG-101 embarked in CV-21. The second one was aboard USS *Kearsarge* (CVA-33) from 11 August 1952 to 17 March 1953, and again the unit was part of CVG-101. Using the 'A' tail code on both deployments, VF-884 logged a combined total of

1519 missions, dropped 750,000 lbs of bombs and fired 1,400,000 rounds of ammunition during the course of the two cruises. A veteran of the first deployment, BuNo 97143 was built in August 1945 and placed in storage until shipped to Japan as an attrition replacement in May 1951. Issued to VF-884 the following month, it returned to Japan in November and was then sent to VF-874, embarked in CV-31 with CVG-102. More combat ensued until the carrier headed home in December and BuNo 97143 was left in Japan. The aircraft then joined VF-653 aboard CV-45 in January 1952, and it returned to California with this unit in August of that year. Assigned to NART Oakland, California, in March 1953 and NART Grosse Ile, Michigan, in October 1955, the F4U-4 was stricken in July 1956.

21

F4U-4B BuNo 82176 of VMF-212, USS *Rendova* (CVE-114), September 1951

VMF-212 was under the control of MAG-33, and the squadron went into action in Korea for the first time on the morning of 20 September 1950 – just five days after the Inchon landings. As with all Marine Corps F4U day fighter squadrons to see combat in the war, VMF-212 flew sorties both from land bases and the flightdecks of light carriers. Its first tour at sea came on *Bataan* from 11 December 1950 through to 5 March 1951, when the unit made way for VMF-312. Whilst operating from carriers, Marine Corps units were able to hit targets as far north as the Yalu River. VMF-212 completed three carrier deployments in total, and this aircraft participated in the second of them aboard *Rendova* from 22 September to 6 December 1951. Built in July 1945, BuNo 82176 served with VBF-75 (1945-46), VMF-212 (1946-47) and VMF-115 (1948), prior to being placed in storage. Issued to VF-54 in January 1951, it was sent to Japan as an attrition replacement six months later and passed on to VMF-212 at Pohang (K-3). Embarked in *Rendova* on 22 September along with the rest of the unit, the aircraft was lost just eight days later when it plunged into the Yellow Sea and sank immediately after take-off. Pilot 1Lt Wayne E Boyles was killed.

22

AU-1 BuNo 129359 of VMA-212, Pyongtaek (K-6), May 1953

In mid-1952, MAG-33 took control of all Marine Corps jet squadrons in-theatre and MAG-12 was made responsible for all piston-engined units, including those equipped with Corsairs and Skyraiders. At the same time all F4U attack squadrons had their designations changed from VMF to VMA, with 'F' for Fighter being replaced by 'A' for Attack – a far more representative designation for the role undertaken by these units since the start of the war. The changes occurred just as the ultimate attack variant of the venerable Corsair was reaching units in Korea. The production version of the XF4U-6, the AU-1 was dedicated to fulfilling the ground attack mission. It featured a more powerful R-2800-83W engine that developed 2300 hp with water injection, an extra pair of rocket rails under the outer wing panels that increased the number of stores pylons to ten, and better protection for the pilot. Just 111 were built, and this example reached VMA-212 in September 1952 – the first AU-1s had been issued to the unit three months earlier. BuNo 129359 served exclusively with the squadron until February 1954, when it was placed in storage at MCAS Iwakuni and subsequently stricken two months later.

23
F4U-4B BuNo 97479 of VMF-214, USS *Sicily* (CVE-118), September 1950
One of the most famous Marine Corps fighter squadrons of World War 2, VMF-214 'Black Sheep' will forever be associated with the Corsair. The unit flew the first Marine F4U strikes of the war on 3 August 1950 when eight of its aircraft launched from *Sicily* and attacked enemy positions in the villages of Chinju and Sinban-ni. VMF-214 made just one carrier deployment during its time in-theatre, being embarked in CVE-118 from 1 August to 13 November 1950. A participant in these early missions, BuNo 97479 was built in August 1946 and served with VF-1B (1946-48) until placed in storage. Issued to VMF-323 in July 1950, the aircraft initially saw combat with this unit from *Badoeng Strait*. Transferred to VMF-214 on 9 September, the fighter lasted just six days with the 'Black Sheep', however, for on the 15th it struck the ground during an attack on an NKPA T-34 tank near Inchon. Pilot Capt William Simpson Jr did not survive the crash.

24
F4U-4B BuNo 62940 of VMF-214, Yonpo (K-27), December 1950
This aircraft was amongst the first Corsairs taken to Korea by VMF-214 in July 1950, and it was flown both from shore bases and *Sicily's* flightdeck. Featuring a rare unit emblem on the cowling, as well as a smaller rendition of the badge near the impressive mission tally, BuNo 62940 was built in December 1946 and served with VMF-311 (1947) and VMF-214 (1947-48), prior to being placed in storage. Returned to the 'Black Sheep' in June 1950, the fighter crash-landed on the airstrip at Koto-ri, in North Korea, on 9 December – pilot Lt Joe R Bibby was uninjured. The aircraft was captured by the enemy when the airstrip was abandoned shortly thereafter.

25
F4U-4 BuNo 97380 of VMF-312, USS *Bataan* (CVL-29), May 1951
VMF-312 operated in Korea under the command of MAG-33 during the first two years of the war. The unit flew its first missions in-theatre on 20 September 1950 from the newly liberated airfield at Kimpo (K-14). VMF-312 was involved, along with VMF-212, in flying strikes against retreating enemy forces from daybreak until last light. It completed

no fewer than five carrier deployments during the conflict, and this aircraft participated in the first of these aboard *Bataan* between 5 March and 6 June 1951. BuNo 97380 was assigned to Pacific War Corsair ace Capt Phil DeLong, who used it on 21 April 1951 to down two of the four Yak-9s that he and his wingman engaged north of Chinnampo harbour. VMF/A-312 was the only Marine Corps F4U day fighter unit to be credited with aerial victories in Korea, its pilots downing five communist aircraft in total. Built in April 1946, BuNo 97380 was immediately placed in storage until March 1948, when it was issued to VA-1A. The aircraft then served with VF-14 (1948-49) and saw combat in Korea with VF-32 in late 1950. It remained in Japan when the latter unit headed for home aboard CV-32 in January 1951, and was issued to VMF-312 as an attrition replacement the following month. Returned to CONUS in August of that year, BuNo 97380 was transferred to VF-884 in May 1952, and the fighter was lost when it crashed into the Pacific Ocean on 19 August 1952 while operating from *Kearsarge* shortly after the unit had embarked in the carrier bound for Korea.

26
F4U-4B BuNo 62927 of VMA-312, Pyongtaek (K-6), September 1952
The last of the aerial victories credited to VMF/A-312 was claimed by Capt Jesse Folmar in this aircraft on 10 September 1952, when he destroyed one of two MiG-15s that had bounced both him and his wingman. Folmar's F4U was in turn shot down by four more MiGs that appeared on the scene just minutes later. The Marine was rescued by a Pyongtaek-based USAF SA-16 soon after he baled out into the sea. Built in December 1946, this aircraft had served with VMF-224 (1947-48), VMF-323 (1948), VMF-312 (1949-50), VMT-2 (1950), VMA-311 (1950), VMF-235 (1950) and VF-53 (1951), prior to being shipped to Japan as an attrition replacement in February 1952. Issued to VMF-212 three months later, BuNo 62927 was passed on to VMA-312 in August 1952 and shot down the following month.

27
F4U-4 BuNo 96845 of VMF-323, USS *Sicily* (CVE-118), June 1951
VMF-323 had sailed to the Far East aboard *Badoeng Strait* in late July 1950 and flew its first missions from the vessel on 6 August. The unit had some of the most elaborate nose art of any Corsair squadron during this period. The rattlesnake emblem was its trademark, but it slowly faded from VMF-323 machines as the conflict wore on due to concerns that the demon-like serpent could provoke communist troops to ill treat captured squadron pilots. BuNo 96845 briefly participated in VMF-323's second, and last, carrier deployment, when the unit embarked in *Sicily* from 5 June to 20 September 1951. Built in July 1945, the aircraft had served with VF-3B (1946-47) and NART Squantum, in Massachusetts (1948),

prior to being placed in storage. Sent to Japan as an attrition replacement in October 1950, it saw combat with VF-54 from CV-45 later that same month. The aircraft returned to Japan when the carrier left Korean waters in December, and it was subsequently passed on to VMF-212. Transferred to VMF-323 in May 1951, BuNo 96845 was badly damaged in a landing accident aboard *Sicily* on 8 June. Shipped back to Japan and then on to California, the aircraft was stricken in October 1951 after being declared uneconomical to repair.

28
AU-1 BuNo 129350 of VMA-323, Pyongtaek (K-6), February 1953
In June 1952, VMF-323 was re-designated just as the first AU-1s started to arrive in-theatre. At this time the unit's complement of 24 Corsairs would have been made up of 12 F4U-4Bs and 12 AU-1s. This particular aircraft was built in April 1952 and issued to VMA-323 at Pyongtaek three months later. Returned to CONUS in March 1954, it served with NART Minneapolis, in Minnesota, until placed in storage in February 1955. BuNo 129350 was stricken in April 1957.

29
F4U-4 BuNo 97466 of VMA-332, USS *Point Cruz* (CVE-119), July 1953
The last Marine Corps Corsair squadron to enter the war was VMA-332, which took over VMA-312's aircraft in Japan in June 1953 and repainted their cowlings with its distinctive 'Polka Dot' pattern. Flying from *Point Cruz*, the unit entered combat shortly thereafter, and remained in-theatre until December 1953. This particular aircraft was built in August 1946 and served with VF-2B (1946-49), prior to seeing combat with VF-114 aboard CV-47 in 1950-51. Issued to VMA-323 in June 1952, BuNo 97466 was transferred to VMA-332 when the former returned to CONUS in early July 1953. Passed on to NART South Weymouth, Massachusetts, in April 1954, the aircraft was retired in October 1955 and stricken in April 1956.

30
F4U-5N BuNo 123176 of VMF(N)-513, Kangnung (K-18), October 1951
The Marines Corps fielded two squadrons of nightfighters in Korea, namely VMF(N)-542 with F7F-3Ns and VMF(N)-513 with F4U-5Ns. The latter unit's Corsairs began using the flat blue/grey finish seen here at about the same time as the frontlines stabilised in the spring of 1951 after the Chinese offensive had been halted. Matt paint proved to be less susceptible to detection by enemy searchlights. All Marine Corps nightfighters had had their white lettering replaced with characters in dull red by mid 1951 too. This particular aircraft was built in September 1949 and issued to VMF(N)-513 in May 1950. Sent to Korea as an attrition replacement in March 1951, the fighter was flying a night mission with a PB-4Y Privateer flare-drop aircraft on 29 October 1951 when it developed engine problems after a strafing run and crashed. Its pilot, 1Lt Donald W Dorn, was killed in the incident.

31
F4U-5N BuNo 123180 of VMF(N)-513, Kangnung (K-18), June 1951
Seen in the original colour scheme worn by VMF(N)-513 for the first year of the war, this aircraft was also built in September 1949 and issued to the unit in May 1950. Sent to Korea in June 1951, the fighter was returning from a night mission on 23 October 1951 when its fuel pump failed near Taegu and pilot Capt George R A Johns was forced to bale out. He was quickly rescued.

32
F4U-5P BuNo 122168 of VMJ-1, Pohang (K-3), August 1952
Marine Corps Photographic Squadron VMJ/F-1 was a vital part of the 1st Marine Aircraft Wing (MAW) in the Korean War. It operated a very small number of F4U-5Ps and F7F-3Ps throughout the conflict, and was later issued with F2H-2P Banshees. A detachment of just two F4U-5Ps, equipped with K-18 cameras, was responsible for filming the various tide levels in Inchon harbour prior to the Marine Corps' amphibious landings on 15 September 1950. This particular aircraft was built in September 1948 and then stored until issued to MAW-2 in August 1950. Briefly allocated to VMF-212 that same month, the Corsair remained with MAW-2 until sent to Japan as an attrition replacement in October 1951. Four months later it was assigned to VMJ-1 (which became VMF-1 in August 1952), and it saw action in Korea until returned to Japan in December 1952. Shipped back to CONUS in February 1953, the aircraft was stored and then stricken in April 1956.

33
F4U-4 BuNo 81865 of MAMRON-33, Pohang (K-3), March 1952
Marine Air Maintenance Squadron 33 was responsible for keeping Korea-based F4Us serviceable. It also operated a small flight of aircraft for MAG-12's Headquarters Squadron, and this machine, christened *THE FIGHTIN' KILROY*, was one such machine. Built in June 1945, BuNo 81865 served with VF-74A (1945), VF-74 (1945-46), VF-1B (1946) and VMF-113 (1947), prior to being stored until late 1950. Shipped to Japan as an attrition replacement in May 1951, the fighter was issued to VMF-323 the following month, and remained with the unit aboard *Sicily* until transferred to MAMRON-33 in November. Routinely flown on combat missions by MAG-12 HQ pilots tagging along with other frontline Marine F4U units at Pohang, BuNo 81865 suffered engine failure shortly after take-off from the base on 1 April 1952. Its pilot, 2Lt Peter Magee of MAG-12, attempted an emergency landing but the fighter crashed heavily and was a total loss. Magee was seriously injured in the incident.

INDEX

References to illustrations are shown in .
Plates are shown with page and caption locators
in brackets.